Girlfriend of a Gangbanger, Inc. Presents Billie's Child

Gail Reed West

ROYSTON
Publishing

BK Royston Publishing
P. O. Box 4321
Jeffersonville, IN 47131
502-802-5385
http://www.bkroystonpublishing.com
bkroystonpublishing@gmail.com

Cover Design: Elite Book Covers
Cover Photo: Nicholas Steward Productions. LLC
Hair and Makeup Artist: TiffiRay @MUA

ISBN-13: 978-1-951941-82-6

Printed in the United States of America

Definitions

gangbanger - an active participant in a particular gang

gang member -a participant who has quite active participation in a set or gang affiliation

hood - a neighborhood, usually in ghettos or in low-income areas, and *slang* for an endearing neighborhood

drug addict - a person who is addicted to illegal and/or prescription drugs

trifling - of very little importance or below society standards (hood definition is nasty)

pedophile - a person who is sexually attracted to children

baby daddy - *slang,* father who is not married, his babies are usually born out of wedlock

sugar daddy - one who lavishes gifts on a young woman for her company and sexual favors, *slang meaning,* a whore.

deliverance - spiritual, when one is taken from the darkness into the light of Jesus Christ and Satan has no more control; he has lost his control of your mind

Holy Ghost - the comforter who is sent by God, to lead and guide you into truth and understanding. John 16:13 Acts 1: 2-3

Jesus Christ as Savior - Christ, to a person whom God has given the revelation that they need a savior from their sins. (the Logos word)

Jesus Christ as King - Christ, to a person whose mind has been luminated to know that Jesus Christ is the Savior of the world.

Jesus Christ as Lord - Christ, to a person who has the inspiration from the Holy Ghost and has made Jesus Lord over their entire lives, *slang,* sold-out

Acknowledgements

GOAGINC.ORG sincerely wishes to thank all my *family and friends* who have prayed, supported, and gave, I appreciate you forever. "God answers prayers."

105th Street and San Pedro, "THE BLOCK" we had the coolest hood in South Central. *(Other than* 111th street) We made the best of where we were and what we had...

To my churches and my pastors, you have endured this journey with me. I am humbled, with a special thanks to East 105st Christian Church, where I found Christ, Greater Bethany Community Church, my father in the faith, the late Honorable Bishop R.W. McMurray, who identified my calling in the body of Christ.

Loveland Church, for spiritual generosity, Power of love, Jeremiah 22, Wind of the Spirit Worship Center, who helped me raise my children.

Redeemed Christian Church - Breakthroughs, Family In Christ Ministries International-My family.

My confidante and friend, Pastor Camelia Joseph, the CEO of Kingdom Works Ministries/The Joseph Group.

Beloved, I wish above all things that you would be in health and prosper, even as your soul prospers. 3 John 1:1

BK Publishing and Julia Royston, you are a Godsend.

Truly, all things work together for good to those who love God, to those who are called according to God's purpose. Romans 8:28

Table of Contents

Foreword

There are no accidents in life...

I first met Gail Reed West one sunny day in July 2020 when she walked in the Family in Christ Ministries International Church business establishment, Family Treasure Box Store in Lancaster, California.

A very courteous lady, she was looking around for something that will catch her eyes. A dress that glitters, an ornate candleholder or any silver accented and artistic home decor she loves anything that defines beauty and harmony.

The next time we've met was in our Sunday morning Church Service. She accepted my prior invitation and at that gathering she led the congregation to a powerful and heartfelt prayer. The people were moved. Gail is a charming woman, witty, graceful, warm, and remarkably erudite. Deeply spiritual, she has great perception and extraordinary prophetic vision, who to say the least lived her life in constant search for the truth no matter how painful it is.

I am excited about BILLIE'S Child because it answered questions about life, laughter and love. It floats between memories and dreams, family and fantasy, visions and her mission.

It resonates with inner power and spiritual strength that interweave with the choices, chances and changes she experienced in her life in the "hood."

Gangs, drugs, Crips, blood, sweat, heartache and tears. Personal, provocative, generous and informative, this is a compelling self-portrait of Gail Reed West's life, love and the testing of her faith. This is a journey of an amazing woman who as a result of God's Grace, the Power of His Word, and the still small voice of the Holy Spirit, went to look at herself in a mirror and see herself as a beautiful child of the King.

Yes it's filled with stories about her trials, troubles and tribulations to make us all understand how life would be without Christ. As the Book of Proverbs 16:25 declared "There is a way that appears to be right, but in the end it leads to death."

Ultimately this book, like a good biographical sketch by itself, should inspire and warm our hearts to reach out and return to God and remain in

Him. Only then can we claim the promises in Romans Chapter 8 verse 28, "And we know that all things work together for good to those who love Him, and who have been called according to His purpose."

Pastor Ruben Ondangan, Jr.
Senior Pastor of Family in Christ Ministries International Church, Incorporated

From a dysfunctional house, to a jailhouse, to the church house, come with me as I take you on my journey, one I wouldn't wish on any girl or woman anywhere. Choices and decisions led me into circumstances that spun a web of deceit and heartache that was meant to destroy my very existence and wipe me out of anything that resembled a good and decent life. I found myself in the depths of darkness and shame, and through that devastation, came a friend and Savior I knew not of, to reveal a compassion and love that was unmistakable. I found Him to be the most 'powerful gangbanger' I've ever known and the baddest brother I've ever met. Anyone who could weave my life back together for good and make all things work together has my unconditional loyalty, love and devotion. This is the story of how my life unfolded. My story is dedicated to gangbangers, gang members, pimps, whores, hustlers, drug addicts, drug dealers, jailhouse wives, all penitentiary inmates, and all abused people everywhere, I know a Man! GIRLFRIEND OF A GANGBANGER INC. presents, Billie's Child.

CONTACT INSTAGRAM @GAILREED

PAYPAL@ GIRLFRIENDOFAGANGBANGER INC

CASHAPP $GAILREEDWEST

-DAVID RAY, JR.

A journey like no other !!! My name is Shu-Shu. I'm the eldest son of the author of this book. We loved our hood. I heard all of the stories of the crips and bloods. I even became a member of main street mafia crips !!!

When I was born in 1974, my mama was in the throes of the lifestyle. She has written about it and my husslin' too. I always kept my family first. I kept my mama first, I'm grateful God kept his eye on the sparrow. I was a product of my environment 'and I loved it!' She nicknamed me Bishop. I'm am honored she calls me friend.

I'm sure this book will make you pause and think about the decisions you're making and the consequences it may bring. I walked this journey with my mother and I also watched her get the victory over hate, a broken heart, a wounded spirit and ultimate betrayal only to emerge as a beautiful black sister who never lost her faith...

She was determined to win with her Lord and Savior Jesus Christ!!!
#goaginc "realtalk" enjoy!

SHU-SHU- #Mainstreetmafia!

-Trivell

– GOAGINC: from a real West LA Blood your son in law or Preacher 'which is your preferred name for me, I've been watching the growth of #GOAGINC. For seven years and seen it come full circle, I'm proud to be a financial blessing to your ministry. Now it's time to give the world a view of your journey and share the healing that has taken place in your life. Now it is your turn moms to show the power you have with The Almighty.

Your views are from lessons, and your words come with power, I know for a fact that everybody who reads this book will find lessons that cost you everything to learn. Some of my best conversations have been with you even when I knew your heart was breaking. Readers will receive a real GOAG perspective, you really been around the world the 3x and seen everybody twice.!!!

Trivell - Trex BityFines!!!!!!

Chapter 1
In the Beginning – Hercy and Sam

Growing up in South Central Los Angeles wasn't so bad. Living through the Watts riots and clearly not understanding why it was so terrifying hearing sirens, ambulance noise, trying to hear clearly the conversations being had about the events surrounding the civil disturbance, one thing was very clear. Looting was the prize and bounty of the uproar, the dead, the wounded, and jailed were a consequence of civil unrest.

Did you know Los Angeles means lost angels? If you're not careful about your life, you'll get swept up in the spirit of Hollywood and gangs and forget it's a business, and to play, you must pay. Your life is not a two-hour movie. It has to be played out scene by scene, and the only person who can call cut is you.

Living on 105th Street, was a step up from the Nickerson Gardens, where we spent a lot of time hanging out with our cousins. Between my mother and her sister, there were fourteen of us, in various age brackets. My mother Billie was an extremely beautiful woman, with Creole skin, shapely bowed legs, and curly soft hair. Of course, when men came into her orbit, they were smitten, doing their best to gain her attention, which inevitably led to her affections. While attending Freemont High School, she met Sam Sr. and boy, oh boy, was he good looking, dark-skinned boy, short in stature, star of the football team, the two became fast lovers, and of course, no sooner than they could sneeze, she was with child.

In the days of *old,* marriage was more what was expected than just having children out of wedlock. In my opinion, Billie wasn't that excited about the union. Nevertheless, they endured a marriage brought on by unwanted pregnancies, a web of madness where neither partner seemed to be committed to the fundamental law of love and certainly not till death do they part.

Sam and Billie endured this strange relationship for a few years. Come to find out, Sam was a major whoremonger to say the least. His appetite for women and underage girls was a fire that burned in his flesh and eventually destroyed his soul and conscience.

My brother Monte was born in April of 1956, and indeed, he was a handsome fella. My mother often said he had issues as a child. He banged his head against the wall until they had to pay close attention to his behavior, or he would bust his head open. Clearly, the boy was bipolar. The next year, I entered the scene, in December of 1957. My brother and I were too young to know or even understand the dynamics of this high dysfunction of two very immature people playing house with kids neither wanted. Both parents were too young and naïve about the commitment and responsibilities of rearing kids.

They finally decided to separate themselves from one another, perhaps due to the bastard of a father and husband he was. Of course, this is my version of the story as I grew up to put two and two together. As a child, I saw my mother in situations with men who frightened me, sometimes thinking her kids were the cause of the problem, or she had no clue of the power she possessed. At four years old we hid in back of a garage, hiding from someone seeking to do us harm, and the smell of oatmeal always brings that memory back. At the same time, in my mind, I was with my mother and I felt strangely okay but terrified. This was the age I remember the most. I was excited about going to school soon. On my first day of school, I passed out books to the whole class. Clearly, I showed early signs of intelligence. I also enjoyed planting yellow roses in the back yard with my mother; the feel of the dirt in my hands was very surreal, learning about bugs and suckers. Now this should have been a time of simple fundamental growth. Unbeknownst to me, things went horribly backward.

Billie met and moved in with a man I'll call Hercy. This relationship would come to define much of my story. My mother had birthed two more children by different baby daddies, prior to her meeting Hercy. So, she went into this relationship with four children. One thing I will say is that my mother gave all her children their fathers' last names. She felt it was a divine right, although she had no religion at this point. It was important to Billie to have her kids in a safe and comfortable environment. Hercy had no children, and she felt this was a suitable arrangement for a prospective stepfather. We were too young to object.

When we moved to 105th San Pedro, we were all so young, and clearly, all we knew was we were with our mother. From the beginning, my stepfather had a serious problem with my brother and I, although I was too young to realize this attitude came from the fact our mother was still married to Sam. That was the way we were raised, with Hercy hating our father and taking it out on us. It was the four of us, in this little circle of a confused family function.

It was also a time of fun. We played ball, water games, house, and went to Dodgers games, my brother being the daddy. As we grew, these games began to develop into something not so childlike anymore, and he wanted to play nasty! So we quit playing with him and found other things to make our little existence worth living. We also had the best block parties in South Central.

The older we got, we figured out what was really going on. It was so cool playing with other kids and making new friends. Friends, we had. It was a block of families, and we had a ball, not knowing these times would bring tragedies, mental illness, sorrows, and at the end of it, we loved and cared for each other!

As we matured, I realized there was something wrong with my mother. I couldn't put it together until I heard talk, I was a nosey child, I saw my mother asleep, sitting in the chair. She nodded and slurred her speech. My stepfather cursed—bad words—and we thought she didn't get enough sleep. Some days, I would clean the house and cook for her, so Hercy wouldn't fuss and curse at her. This behavior would continue for years. We just dealt with it, and since I was the oldest girl, the pressure was on me to do certain things. Of course, that meant something was going to suffer. The first thing was school; I took absolutely no interest in it. Everything began to suffer for me. My mother was present but not there. There was no guidance, no one to tell me how to become a young lady. I surely would pay for not having the right start. My two sisters didn't struggle with this, but it would become my biggest challenge on my journey called unscripted life.

Chapter 2
RAYMOND WASHINGTON AND D-BOB

105th Street was the block of blocks, nestled in the city of Los Angeles, south of Century, north of Imperial Highway and between Main and San Pedro.

A city filled with life and expectation, no matter who you are and where you fit in. You fit in, poor, middle class, upper class, the spirit of LA is palatable. You can feel the power of the spirits that control the atmosphere, good ones, bad ones; you become intoxicated.

It's a thing that makes people love California and not leave, as dirty as it is now. When you think of where you were placed in the scheme of things, you make the best of what you have. We did that.

I started having sex in my early teens. My age didn't matter, and if that meant sex was going to get love for me, so be it. I wanted love, and that meant anywhere I could find it. Not really getting the attention I needed from home, I looked for it elsewhere. Since I was the lost sheep of the bunch, I knew I had to do whatever I could to get attention, and attention I sought. I had already been molested by the age of seven, by men who should have been protecting me.

The first boy I locked my eyes on was nineteen, when I was thirteen. I'll call him Tony. I sat in the front window of our house and watched him pass by when he visited his sister's house. I listened to Rolls Royce and daydreamed. I was really wishing on a star. To me, he was good-looking, and I knew early on, I liked good-looking men. One sunny day, I got bold enough to give him a letter, to let him know how I felt. This was some serious bullshit; I was in some fairytale that either I thought up or saw on TV. I remember ditching twenty-eight days of school to go to his apartment on Hooper Street, and no one from Gompers Jr.

High School never called my house and told my mama, and if they did call, she probably was so high she didn't even bother. This was the beginning of what would be the losing of my soul.

By this time, I was hitting fourteen. Mama wasn't paying any attention; she and Hercy were doing their own thing, waiting for the weekend. By this time, my brother was living with Sam. He had ran away to LAX the airport and slept on benches. The next day, he called Mama and told her she kept letting Hercy beat on us, and he wasn't taking any more ass whipping. So Mama called Sam, and that's how Monte moved off 105th Street, the block.

Monte moved with Sam on 76th Street Central. This boy was book-smart, straight A's, but that wasn't good enough. He simply didn't like school. The girls loved him because he was a very handsome young man. It seemed he needed more excitement. One day while Monte was walking his dog Sheba, which was a Great Dane, Raymond Washington approached him and threatened to kick his dog's ass.

Monte replied, not knowing who he was, "I'll tie him up and kick your ass if you touch this dog." It was history after that. Monte became an *East Side Crip.*

1973, it was fist fights. A lot of dudes would get together at the surrounding schools, Locke, Freemont, Washington, and many others, and have scrimmages and fights. There would be shooting as well, and it was around this time, things were getting worse. Gangs were being established— Bloods, Hoovers, Piru, West side Crips, Q102. Sets sparked up everywhere; you just couldn't keep count.

It was clear that the line in the sand was drawn, and you had to choose. Most of it was decided by where you lived. The boundaries were clearly an issue. You could get stopped and you had to say what set you were from and that answer could cost you your life. Sometimes you would get a pass if the Lord was with you, and you hoped and prayed he was. It didn't matter if you wanted to be a part of it or not, many times brothers got caught up in the drama by reason of Geographic's, my other brothers got a pass because of Monte.

It was the summer of 1972, and we all were preparing for the summer—what boys we were going to screw, what beaches we would crash. One weekend, Monte came to visit us on 105th Street. He brought Raymond Washington with him. At first, meeting him, it was lost on us who he was. They started playing drums on our back porch, and my sisters and I sat and listened.

Later that week, Raymond W came back alone and asked if he could talk to me. By this time, we all were well aware of who he was. He asked if I would be his girlfriend; now, I didn't say yes, but I didn't say no. I, being a low level hustler, thought very carefully about how this could benefit me and how it would give street creds. Although I refused to be a Cripalet, I needed money and I had the most popular boyfriend. It was settled. The word got out. I was his girlfriend, and so it was, I was the girlfriend of the notorious leader of the Los Angeles Crips.

Every week, he would bring me gifts and money. It kind of blew my mind, but I took them. After all, nobody had ever talked to me about boys and what you do and what you don't do.

One August evening, we went driving around town, and gunshots rang out from our car. We were five deep, and this really bothered me, the fact that I was so naïve. I thought about it hard, so I listened to the news, and there was no coverage of someone getting shot. Since I was sitting in the middle and it was dark outside, I couldn't see if they actually hit someone, but that's when it became clear, these guys were FOR-REAL GANGBANGERS!

I never thought about why I felt the need to hang with people like this. Maybe it was because I wasn't getting any attention at home. Well, I was getting the attention I didn't want, like if I did something wrong, attention was well paid with belts and extension cords. As a teenage girl, I wished my mother would have disciplined me. At least, it would have come from a place of love. Although my mother was a heroin addict, we knew she loved us. She married Hercy to give us a roof over our heads, clothes on our back, and food on the table every night. However, sometimes I wish she would have made herself happy. That's obviously coming from a place of watching her suffer. I can't imagine having sex with a man I didn't love NOW.

Raymond was getting more popular in the Crips. They were on the police radar, and we knew it. We really weren't afraid of the police back then;

maybe we should have been. They say 'youth is wasted on the young' and it's the truth.

A lot of killings were jumping off. One evening. my friend Jacie and I were with Raymond, on 118th Street. We all were on the porch talking, and a car came by, spraying bullets. Shooting broke out, and I, being so naïve, didn't know what was really going on. Raymond took my head and threw me to the ground. Now, it was clear to me, in that moment, they were killing each other, and I was in the mix.

When the news got back to my brother, he forbade me to go with Raymond W again, but his advice fell on deaf ears. After all, Raymond was giving me money, and I wanted that. We went to his mother's house on 76th Street, to consummate the fact we were boyfriend and girlfriend. It was very uneventful, but the deed was done. I didn't hear from him in a while, and it was told to me he caught a case and was doing time in Tracy Penitentiary. He got my address from somewhere and began writing letters. I received a letter a day. The postman would tease me that 'here's a letter from that nigger.' At the same time, he trying to get a rub of my breast. He truly was a pervert. The postman would later tell me he would give me my county check early if he could rub my breast, and I let him.

By this time, I was going to Freemont High School; not that I was going to school, but it was different. My cousin Yvonne was going there, and it was a new adventure. One day, everybody was getting a ride home and I didn't have one, so a friend of ours got me a ride with a boy named "aka" D-Bob. When I opened the door, there were box carts. I had to sit on box carts. Now it had a pretty paint job, burnt orange. I focused my attention on how good-looking he was, and I do mean fine. As we drove to 105th Street, he started asking me questions. He was different than

Raymond. I liked the way he looked. He was tall, handsome and the kind of man silly girls dream of.

When we drove up to my house, he asked me if I wanted to be his girlfriend, and I had to let him know in one hour and fifteen minutes, so I gave him my number.

Well, I knew I didn't want to let him out of my sight. I had to say something, and I was too stupid not to make him wait. I didn't have any self-worth, and I didn't think enough of myself to determine what his motive was. One week later, I brought him home to meet my mother. We found her sleeping on the sofa, and when I introduced him, she raised up out of her induced state of euphoria and politely said, "Get that nigger out of here; he ain't worth a shit." I was stunned. My mama usually liked people; however, she was sure about him.

Well, I didn't pay that any mind because I couldn't take anything too serious. I was pretty much on my own at fifteen. We starting having sex all over the place. It was like I couldn't get enough, and this behavior went on for months. Well, finally my mother got wind of it, but it was too late. I was pregnant—oh boy, good and with child.

When Hercy and Mama had our 'come to Jesus' meeting, Hercy said he was going to whip me for my rebellion and trifling ways. This time, I stood up and answered him, "THERE WILL BE NO MORE WHIPPINS!" And from that day forward, it was as I said and as I wanted.

D-bob denied the baby. What the hell? I was so humiliated, so crushed, so embarrassed, then two weeks later, my mama told me that another girl was pregnant as well. I couldn't believe it, but it was true. Her name was Barbie Doll, and she lived on 80th Street San Pedro so I made it my business to find out who this was. Sure enough, well, it was true, and our bellies looked alike! My mother's words hit me like a hammer. He wasn't worth it. She explained that I had given my life to someone who did not feel like I felt. My feelings were clear; I loved him.

I was fixed on the fact that I had competition. I just wanted to see what see looked like. I wanted her to look like a dog, and I pretty much got my wish, but she had him. She had his heart, and the rest didn't matter. I had just been handed a lesson of my life—looks ain't worth a darn if your heart is broken. I remembered Raymond Washington telling me I was a pretty girl. Pretty, and don't ever give a man money or become a prostitute, never let anyone tell me different. I guess I started to believe it or should have! I started making my myself as pretty as I could, to win his attention. All it got was second; then, come to find out, I was third.

I had to go the hall of records to get the birth certificate. My mama let us use her car and D-Bob drove. When I asked for my child's birth records, they kept asking me if my name was Barbie Doll. I told the clerk my name and my son's name, and he told me all he had was a birth record for a D.M. Roberts. The mother's name was Barbie Doll, and the child was born on March 13, in Adams Hospital. I was, again, crushed to the bone. He named both sons D-Bob, twelve days apart in age, and the only reason we were at different hospitals was because I had changed doctors.

We went on for years with this drama, and I was pretty tired of it all. I started seeing other people. By this time, there was a lot of gang activity in the hood, and Q102 Crips had put a snitch jacket on D-Bob. That was as bad as it can get, by reputation standards, in the hood. They had a contract to kill him, and stupid me, I'm standing by my man, but the police wouldn't let me sit in court and listen to him testify against his homeys. Wonder why his other two girlfriends weren't around? They weren't one of Raymond Washington's exes that's the only reason D-bob wanted me in court.

By this time, Raymond was released from prison. He came to 105th Street and couldn't wait to tell me he had taken the contract off my baby daddy and *me*. Me! I didn't snitch! He told me he wasn't angry at me for having my son. I really didn't care if he was angry. It was love driving my relationship, however misguided it was. To tell the truth, I was a little nervous about what his reaction would be, and because I knew he cared about me, he hit one of his friends for calling me ugly, knocked him clean out. My reaction was *wow*! I liked him; it looked as if it hurt really bad.

On a Monday in February, my 'other' boyfriend brought me a car, a stick shift Vega, so I could get to school. I had decided to improve myself. He took me to fancy restaurants where I ate things like frog legs and escargot. Anyway, D-Bob spent the night at my apt on 90th Vermont. There was a knock at the door, and sure enough, it was Barbie Doll. She made him jump up and get out of the bed, and chase her down the street. So I got in my car and followed them. I told him to get in the car. In fact, I pleaded, and I pleaded, but of course, my pleas went unheeded. Still with no self-dignity, I drove all the way to 113th, and there was a bridge over the freeway. I looked at D-bob and told him if he crossed that bridge with her, we were through. HE CROSSED THE BRIDGE, so I drove to the other side and invited them to get in the car and I would take them wherever they were going. They got in, just as if we were one big, happy family. Three years later, he asked me to marry him, and even got my mother involved. She encouraged the marriage for the sake of her grandson. When I said no, he replied, "I crossed the bridge," and I said, "You crossed the bridge."

Chapter 3
If I Only Had a Daddy

I knew in writing this chapter, it would probably offend. Nevertheless, I'll take this liberty as his oldest daughter, the only child conceived and born in wedlock. You say that today, they would probably say what's that? I don't intentionally intend to hurt any, but some truths you need to hear to set you free.

Sam was a very handsome man; any woman who met him was attracted to him. My mom left him early in their marriage. Later in life, I learned why. He couldn't keep his hands off women and girls. Mama never told me what he actually did until a week before she died.

One day, I asked my father to go find me a car a *bucket* I gave him my $2000.00. I felt I could get a pretty decent car for that price in 1982. He took the money, and I expected to hear from him within a week or so. When two weeks had passed, I went over to his house on 110th Street. I knocked on the door. No one answered, but the back door was open. What the hell did I smell but sex! So as I was about to leave, he came out of the room. I knew his wife was at work, but I didn't want to make waves, until I saw his stepdaughter come out behind him. I WAS HORRIFED. I asked for my money back, as I was walking out the door, he reached for my arm, slammed me to the ground and beat the hell of me for catching him in the act of child molestation. I told him to just give me my money. I finally got away from him. I hurried and went to my mama's house on the block and told her everything he had done. And that was all she wrote. Mama put me in a car and took me back down to his house. I didn't know she had her thirty-eight pistol; she went in the back door without knocking, put that thirty-eight to his head and told him if he ever put his hands on me again, she would kill him. She told him he had never put a piece of bread in my mouth, and he had better ever put hands on me as long as he lived. And he gave Mama $1500.00 of the $2000.00 I had given him real quick. I often wondered why mama didn't stop Hercy from those whippings. Then I figured it out Hercy was putting bread in our mouth.....I got all kinds of revelations that day my father was a pedophile, and I knew why my Mama left him, I Looked at my mama's face, and she was not playing. I had never seen Mama that angry. I didn't know he had never put a piece of bread in my mouth. Hell, I sure wouldn't have given him my money if I had known.

Well, one month later, he showed up at my house on Broadway and tried to apologize for his behavior. Only thing, I was high on sherm stick, and wouldn't you know, I saw in his eyes, if he could have taken advantage of me, he would have. I knew just like I knew my name. I didn't know God, but something kept him from touching me that day, and I knew it. Later, God would reveal why.

Unfortunately, I didn't have contact with him again until 1988. Sadly, I wanted to stay as far away from him as possible. The things I had learned about my father scared me. Although I had been molested at seven, it wasn't my fault, so where did this promiscuous spirit come from? Why was I so quick to want to give sex to men, to make them like or want me? Did it come from a place I had no knowledge of? When I saw him again, I was told he was up to his old tricks.

The story is my brother Monte had this girlfriend named Candy, and he was crazy about her. Somehow, Sam met this girl and began to finagle his way into Candy's life. The next thing I heard, she was Sam's woman—oh dam here he go again, I watched how this affected my brother, even though they shared women all the time. But I guess he really liked this one. Well, a lot of kids came through this relationship. Sam Jr. said the first boy was his. The only problem is Sam Sr. had Candy on the hoe stroll—you can't make this stuff up. All six of the kids look like Mexicans, and I love them all. HELLO!

I started seeing my brother Monte go downhill after that. One thing I will say about when he was boss of the neighborhood, he was boss and had much respect, kind of like "Nipsey" and every bit a Crip. My brother was smart. He didn't have to study for tests; he just knew the work. He was the only one of mama's kids who had that sharp book-brain. The rest of us had to study, some more than others.

When you are thirteen, the world is yours, or so you think, especially when you don't have many rules and regulations. You are trying to find your style, something that's going to make you stand out and be popular. Boys were everywhere, and I *liked* boys, no matter if they where they were.

Since I had already been molested as a child, I knew what boys wanted, and I wanted to give it to them. I told you about the nineteen year old, well, that was getting old, and I was looking to get fresh meat.

I didn't see myself as pretty or cute. In fact, I was a bit trifling. The boys I liked didn't like me. They were fine, and they had cars and money, so I told them I was fifteen, like that's much different. Since I couldn't have the boys I liked, I went out of the neighborhood to find attention,

It was Christmas time and all the lights and trees were up. It was easy to go do dirt; my parents were drunk and high, enjoying the holiday spirits— literally!

I had met this boy named Michael, and he was tall, brown, not so cute, but he was my brother's friend. We talked for a few days, and then we found a spot and got busy. The next day, he told everybody I peed in the bed and wrote it on the church wall—that SOB—and it stayed there for what looked like years. I didn't give a damn; my brother should have taken it down. I wet the bed until I was fifteen. Now what? Most of us slept around with ignorant boys Locke High School was where we hung out, dice games ditching parties, and some of us even went to school. Needless to say, I hated school.

Between Hercy and Mama, with their drunken and heroin highs, I lived contently in my daydreams I would find a good looking, strong boyfriends and he would take me away from this shit. In my mind, there was nothing else.

I wrote notes, excusing my brothers and sisters from school, so we all could go on a trip somewhere beautiful and fun. Well, the reality set in fast, as soon as something wasn't done. Here came Hercy with that extension cord, and he beat us with it unmercifully, Monte and me. My two sisters were spared. Remember, Sam wasn't their father. My stepfather hated Sam, so he hated us!

I went to Locke High School to enroll in the drill team, and I was still at Gompers, trying to be in with the special people. Even Patrice Rushen was playing for Gompers Jr. High and Locke High School

Well, I didn't get on the drill team, so I started looking for something else to occupy my time.

111PL and San Pedro was full of activity. All the brothers with nice cars, low riders, and all the girls were there. There went my chances of getting who I wanted. My clothes were never right, and sometimes I would get teased and laughed at.

There was a mother on that block who I thought was a beautiful woman. She looked like a queen; her name was Grace. Ms. Grace had class, beauty, style, charm, and a beautiful body. If I could have had her teach me about the game, I would have been fearless. I knew she could, but she had hundreds of people at her house, every weekend. She had five kids, and they were all popular. I'm going to name one of the sons I just adored. His name was Mikel. Unfortunately, he died from a gunshot by his baby mama's sister, come to find out Ms. Grace was the weed dealer, she didn't have to go far for her clientele.

Chapter 4
Sugar Daddy and Sugar Daddy Jr.

One day, while minding my own business driving down 104th and Gramercy, a car hit me. I was in my mother's car, and there was a witness who saw the accident. Clearly, I had the right of way. The other driver was a preacher, and he was drunk. The witness' name was Mr. Green, and he confirmed that the preacher was in the wrong. Little did I know, Mr. Green was eyeballing me. This was new to me. I had heard of women having sugar daddies, how they kept them, how they made sure their other woman had what she needed. He gave me his phone number, and I gave him mine.

Later that day, he called and wanted to tell my mama the accident wasn't my fault. Surely, I was grateful he did that. When I took the phone back, he asked how was I doing and would I like to go out to dinner. I was nineteen, and he was around fifty. I thought about it for about a second and decided I would go.

We went to a Moroccan restaurant up in San Pedro; I had not been exposed to things quite like this. The hook was in. Let me add, he was a very good-looking man, with salt and pepper hair, short, a little heavy, but he wore his clothes well, and he had the bucks. He owned a boys' home, property, and a pharmacy; it was a step up from what I was used to. He wined and dined me, and I liked him. I wasn't quite ready to be a personal whore, but he kept buying me things, and he even offered to buy me a new car.

Now, I didn't consider how this would affect my self-esteem. I just rolled with it. He started coming on the block more and more. We would sit and talk, and he would tell me about his family. About a month into our friendship, he wanted to have sex. I knew, eventually, it would come to this. The question was if I was going to start something I couldn't finish. Well, I did, and I did not like it.

Eventually, I just accepted it, and I knew at least I would have to endure this. I felt dirty every time he touched me. The money and the drugs were plenty; nobody complained about the age difference. He gave everybody what they wanted, as long as he could have sex with his nineteen year old naïve, fine young woman, with me not realizing I was selling myself short. This went on for some time, and I was sinking deeper and deeper into a devil's web that only God could bring me out of, and I didn't know Him.

One summer, he brought his friend over, along with a bag of cocaine. We freebased it up. I didn't know they wanted an orgy. The drugs kept coming, so the sex was easy. This happened many times, even with women. It didn't matter; at least with them, he gave us a thousand dollars to perform.

I began to ask myself, *do you want to keep feeling nasty?* it was filth; soap and water couldn't wash away orgies and shit like that. I slowed up for a while, to get control of my trifling behavior.

Later that summer, we met up at a fancy restaurant. He had a friend with him whose name was Will. Will was very charming. He quickly took a liking to me, and I to him. We exchanged numbers. I didn't think to get Mr. Green's permission.

About a week later, we met up and had good conversation. This went on for about two months, and Will was getting serious. He took me to his home, and it was super nice. We stayed all night, and I enjoyed myself, finally having sex with someone I liked.

Later in the fall, Lloyd—Mr. Green—found out Will and I were dating. Clearly, I had neglected to tell him. Will asked Mr. Green questions about me personally. What the hell could he say that was favorable? NOTHING!!!

Needless to say, he was furious. He cursed me out and told me he didn't care if I married Will, I would always be his BITCH! That's when he wanted sex. I would have to submit, or he would tell Will about me and him. What the hell was I looking at? I couldn't believe he thought he had that much control, and as far as I was concerned, he didn't.

Later that week, I told Mr. Green it was over, that I liked Will and we were going to get married. Why did I say that? The next day, Will told me everything was over and not to call him again. As far as Mr. Green was concerned, he was a wicked devil and tied to gangsters, for real, and Will wanted no part in it.

I was mad as hell. Here, I had a chance at happiness, and he stepped in and told that man everything we had been doing. I stayed upset for a while, until the drugs and cash got low, and I called him. He came with loads of drugs, and it started all over again. For some strange reason, Mama liked Mr. Green; he was exceptionally nice to her.

Mr. Green was going up north to visit his son, so I asked him if I could come and visit my best cousin Lynn, in Oakland, California. My BFF decided to go with me to see her folks, in Richmond, California.

Mr. Green always had a brand new Cadillac, and we drove up at night. When we got close to San Jose, Mr. Green told us we would have to wait at Denny's, because his son was married and we couldn't go to the house. And so it was; we waited. When they came to get us, he had his son in the driver's seat. We all got in the car, headed to Oakland, and all the men were going fishing.

I had Diana Ross playing on the 8-track, and it was sounding good on stereo. My BFF, in the backseat, kept nudging me. I asked her what, why was she nudging me for the third time? She was telling me to look at his son and how fine he was. Not paying attention, I finally took a good look. My BFF knew what I liked and that I would go for it. Wow, why wasn't I paying attention? He *was* fine! I mean gorgeous. I didn't take a second thought. It was 1:00 am, Diana Ross was playing on the stereo, and I started rubbing my fingers through his hair, looking real close at what I had obviously overlooked, and he was charming. Now, I remember Mr. Green telling me many times that he wanted me to take his son away from his wife, because she was too trifling for the family name. "What the hell?" I remember replying. I'm trifling too, remember, and NEVER gave it a second thought. He even offered me money, imagine that! I would always reply, "I'm no different."

So we got closer to my cousin's house in Oakland, and he looked at me with a stern face and a strong beautiful voice and said, "Don't start what you can't finish."

I just laughed and said, "The game is on!"

When we got to my cousin's, we all went in, had drinks, and they left. We stayed all day. When they came back, lo and behold, who came back with Lloyd Sr.? I was shocked that my charms had worked so fast on Lloyd Jr. I thought he was going fishing for the weekend.

We drove back to San Jose, to a hotel. I was not paying attention and didn't care that his daddy had a problem. Junior asked me if he could come back that night and take me to dinner, and of course, I said yes.

When it dawned on me that this is what Lloyd Sr. had been weaving this plot for a long time and probably plotting. I pushed those thoughts aside and found my own truth. I liked him, and if he was happy in his marriage, why was he asking to go on a date with me?

My BFF lent me her mink coat that she had stolen, and I had my own diamonds, snake skin shoes, and my suit, all beige.

Mr. Green was conspicuously silent. I went anyway. I really was having a wonderful time. He made feel like I was the only woman important to him, and we talked for hours. We left the restaurant and pulled up to the lake. Then came the big question. He asked me if I was his daddy's woman! Damn! Damn! Damn! Why did he ask me that question? Now, I had come with his daddy, but I really didn't want to answer that question. He was dead silent as he waited for an answer, and all I was thinking was I wanted to be in this man's life. I looked him in the face and told him a straight, "No!"

Yes, I did, and I was ready to accept whatever came with that answer. From there, we went to a motel, and didn't I get the shock of my life! He screwed just like his daddy. That blew my mind. I tried to keep it together. Believe it or not, it was a turn off for me, but I liked him. He took me to his dorm, where he was president of his fraternity, he carried me upstairs and had me sit in middle of a circle, where all the guys introduced themselves. One got up and told his name and sat down, and one by one, they all did the same. It was blowing my mind. I NEVER gave it a second thought.

We went back to the hotel where everyone was staying. I was in a fog of infatuation and I liked it. We all headed back to Los Angeles. It didn't take long for him to reach out to me. He said he was coming to LA, coming to see me while he was here, and I looked forward to it. He had become special in my mind, and I wanted it to stay that way. Well he came to the house, we dined and had some tequila, and, well, you know the rest. When the morning came, it was hard waking him up. I mean *hard.* I had never seen anyone sleep that deeply. Finally, he woke and asked me if I would consider moving up north, closer to him. He said he wouldn't be in his marriage long, and he wanted me nearby. And he would pay the rent.

So three weeks later, I packed and left, but not before Mr. Green came by the house and had the nerve to tell me that he wanted me to marry his son. I still would have to give him some cock, and he meant that, that dirty son of a bitch. I told him I didn't care what he said, and I was doing it, movin'.

Off to Oakland I went. I found an apartment on 15th Street, off Foothill, a nice place, one bedroom, furnished. I was down there about two weeks when Lloyd Jr. called and asked me to come to his house in San Jose. He assured me it was safe. So I went, and the first thing I noticed were the boxes of things stacked up, lots of boxes. He kept trying to get me to go upstairs, and I refused. I was in the woman's house, I wasn't going to her bed, no matter how much he insisted.

The evening was over, and before I left, he said he was going to be free soon and he would come and get me. I left that day, thinking I was going to start a new life with him, and I was okay with the situation.

It was time for my sister's graduation, and I didn't want to miss that, so I put Shu in the car and headed to LA, but not before I gave my keys to my cousin Lynn. I told her I would be back because my honey and I were headed for our future.

I lingered at my mama's house. One week passed, then two, then three. Lynn wanted to know if I was coming back because she needed to tell the landlord. While watching TV and eating some noodles, the news was on, and they said eight people had burned up in a fire. I heard it but didn't pay much attention to it until Mama came rushing up the stairs completely out of breath and told me that it was Lloyd Jr. and everyone else in the family, except the mother, I was quietly stunned and in utter disbelief, I really didn't know how to feel, I could feel angels driving my car for me. My cousin Lynn in Oakland told me he had called the day after I left and wanted to know where I was. She said she told him I was in LA and would be back soon. I felt like a dead woman, a zombie. How could this happen? All I wanted to do was get to Mr. Lloyd Green Sr. and find out what had happened and what went horrible wrong!

It would take me a week, but I came up with a scheme. I went to the family house and played it off like I was a mourner and got in to see Mr. Green, I could see on his face, he was defeated, crushed. He had worshiped his son and would have done anything for him, including murder. I asked him how he was holding up. He said he didn't really know, and for the first time, I felt sorry for him, even with all the dirty things he had done to others, and I do mean dirty.

He told me he suspected foul play, because his son had told him that he and I were going to be married and he had filed for his divorce. The fireman report said it was someone smoking cigarettes downstairs and the clutter in the house made the flames go quick needless to say I just couldn't handle that news right then; it was too much guilt. I left the family house and tried to think about what the hell had happened. I thought about how he'd tried to get me up those stairs and in their bed. I thought about how cluttered the house was, but nothing brought me release.

I stopped the drugs for a while. I thanked God for protecting me, when I learned he was upstairs at the window with his children I was mortified—what if I had gone up those stairs? I didn't know God then, but He knew me. I was grateful for small things, and I felt something was keeping me from losing my natural mind.

I tried to pull it together for the funeral service in Inglewood, California. I did attend, my beautiful cousin Katy from across the street went with me, it was scary and surreal their they all were six caskets, I didn't want to believe this was happening, but it was, and it was front and center. It was my life staring me in the face, and I didn't know whether I was coming or going. That part was over, so I tried to get out of there. There was no way I was going back to Oakland. I was home. and I was glad I was at Mama's when it happened. That probably saved my sanity.

About a month went by Mr. L Green Sr. came by Mama's house and said they had taken a trip to the Mediterranean, to get their emotions under control and settle their hearts. Too bad I couldn't do that. I had to settle my grief with drugs. Yes, they were back, and when he came, the drugs came too. It was getting progressively worse.

I resumed a sexual relationship with Mr. Green, which was the worst thing I could have done. I would think of Lloyd Jr. just to get through it. This went on for four more years, and I was losing my mind, thinking about Lloyd Jr. and what we had talked about. Every time the date came around, I would freak out on that sherm. I would think my house was on fire, and I had crazy dreams. I was sinking deeper and deeper. I knew I was headed for the graveyard. My mind would flash back to his dead son. This was wicked, terribly wicked.

Chapter 5
Bill II

There was a death in our family; one of our revered uncles died, and everyone was expected to attend the services. They came from Louisiana and Oakland, to honor this life. We arrived at the graveyard to bury our family member, and this brother in the distance across the graveyard had my attention. Oh, my goodness, I saw what I wanted and I was going to get what I needed. I determined, in my mind, I was going to get his attention one way or another. When we went to the family house to have the repast dinner, I was sitting in the guest room eating, getting away from everyone to work out a plan to get his attention.

Then I saw him coming out of the restroom, and he looked over in my direction. I asked him to come over and let me talk to him. He was quick to oblige me and sat down on the bed and introduced himself. We began small talk, and I knew right away, he wouldn't be too difficult. They say some woman are easy, but sometimes both the man and the woman are just after the animal attraction of SEX. Well, I began feeding him from my plate, a little at a time. This went on for hours. I really liked his conversation. He didn't talk like a brother from the hood; he was very intelligent in his demeanor, and his clothes were fine. It was getting late, and we were becoming quite obvious. Everyone was curious about the newfound friendship.

We made a date to meet at my house at 8:00. It was a Friday night, and my cousin Lynn was here from Oakland, for the funeral service. I purposely didn't tell her I had just met him. I had my reasons. When he came to my apartment on 90th and Broadway, we sat in the living room and had small talk. Lynn retreated to the bedroom to talk to her beautiful husband.

He invited us to eat dinner at a restaurant of our choice. We were a bit leery because we didn't know what kind of money he had. Of course, we were prepared to go Dutch, but that's a bit tacky.

We went to Red Lobster to dine, and when Bill II pulled out his bankroll to pay the check, *it was a bankroll indeed!* It was sheer genius I had kept the conversation as if we had met before. She surely would have judged me!! When we went back to my place, we talked for hours. He tried to get me to give it up that night, but I kept my cool. Well, Lynn was there, and she was a cock-block for sure.

We had been seeing each other for a few months when he told me he and his wife were separated. At this time, I had one son Shu Shu' and I was feeling maternal. I thought I was a little safe, since I came out of the fog of D- Bob, so I got pregnant with my son Bill III. He was furious and told me he didn't want me to have his children. I was shocked and devastated he didn't want the baby. I was reliving the same bullshit I was living with before. I thought I was smarter. Well, clearly, I wasn't smart at all. I had misjudged this whole relationship, and I was the one left with a baby only I wanted, again.

The slowdown began as quickly as it began it was already showing 'signs of defeat!' with fewer and fewer visits. My mother met him, and she liked him enough. She thought he was a bit different from the rest, but she thought he wouldn't be committed to the relationship.

It got to the point I would drive around to find him at the junkyards where he hung out, and he would be embarrassed that I came. When my son was born, we needed a refrigerator and he brought one over. That would be the last thing we ever received from him. Bill III was a beautiful boy and highly intelligent.

By this time, my sugar daddy had been supplying all the drugs I needed, and I was a stoned drug addict—sherm/pcp, crack cocaine, pills. He owned a pharmacy, and as long as I was giving him some cock he gave me drugs. Bill II would come by the house, and I would be so high, sometimes I couldn't talk. The sherm would have me talking in devil tongues. I preferred sherm to smokin' crack. I was the epitome of a dumb drug addict, and it was one unholy mess. I was so hurt and deprived of self-control; I didn't care. I just couldn't get it together. Everyone in my life was concerned, but I was stubborn, not willin' to admit another mistake.

Well, it was now April 25th 1983, and Bill brought Billy III a birthday present. I was high again. I invited him to come in. I knew he liked playing cards and ponies (Nagas) so I told him we would play a game of Tunk and if I won, we would have sex, and if he won, we wouldn't. I was tired of him lecturing me about being loaded, and good sex would take all the bad feelings away. When he dealt the cards, I double-tunked *on the first card pulled*. I won, so it was on. During the intercourse, he let out this loud sound, and it scared the hell out of me. I thought he was an animal, but he said it was just good sex. Imagine that!!!

It returned to the same thing, but one thing was different. I was pregnant with another child, and this was not good news. I had determined that I wouldn't bring another child into this mess and I meant that. I made an appointment with the abortion clinic for 7:00 am on a Tuesday morning. The things I'm writing really happened, so bear with me. During the night, I was spiritually troubled. Something was wrong; I had an unusual fear in my soul. I heard something, or someone say, **"You will not have the abortion. You have had six, and if you have this one, you will surely die with her."** I was so frightened, so scared! I couldn't figure out who or what had said this. Only I knew I'd had six abortions. I had misused them as a form of birth control or I just didn't know who the daddy was?

While I was trying to figure it out, the phone rang to confirm my 7:00 am appointment, and my bones shook. A fear came over me that I couldn't control. I was too scared to answer, so I didn't.

I finally was up against a power I knew not of! This encounter is when I met Jesus Christ during the pregnancy, and it became a very profound relationship; he had my undivided attention. This Jesus was blowing my natural mind.

Mama starting taking me to a Bible study group on Wednesdays at 12:00 pm, at Sister Ann's house on 84th Street. Little did I know, Mama had made a deal with God—if he would save me, she would put the heroin down. SHE DID! I AM!

So Rachel was born January 8 and she is a pistol. Believe me, she's been a challenge since conception.

Ten days after she was born, she began showing signs of illness. I felt so bad that I had used so many drugs up until I was two months pregnant. Nevertheless, she was ill. I had been hearing the Word and trying to understand who this Jesus was. How do I begin to understand the Bible?

I took her to the doctor's office in Inglewood, California. The doctor insisted there was nothing wrong. I told him he needed to do more tests. He finally did a spinal tap for meningitis, and the fluid came back black. He sat down in disbelief. She was dying. He said if I would have left her home one more day, she would have died.

When she was in the hospital, they had to shave her beautiful hair. Every day, I would see different needles in her head and feet. I was so intimated by the sterile surroundings I was in. I was so dirty. I didn't know how to respond, because I felt guilty. Why would the Spirit forbid an abortion, only to kill her at this point? Well, I determined that I would test this new Jesus who had interrupted my life BY FORCE!

It was a Sunday morning, and I said a prayer early that morning, asking God if he's going to take her. If not, I would use the words in his Bible to speak about her condition. I was naïve about everything, but that Sunday, I read in the Bible and found a scripture in **Mark 5:22-2. One of the church officials named Jairus came up, and on seeing him, I fell at his feet and implored him earnestly, saying, "My little daughter is at the point of death; please come and lay your hands on her so she will live."** I took it literally.

When I finally arrived at the hospital, I was looking at her in the incubator, and there was that voice again. The Spirit said, **"She is healed."**

I almost started shouting and screaming right there in the neonatal ward, so I took the little red Bible book track out of my purse and taped it to the incubator. I told them, "No one touches this, so 'let it be written so let be done'." The doctor said it was my insistence that made him uncomfortable about sending her home

She remained in Centinela Hospital until Valentine's Day. The doctor who treated her called me personally to tell me he admired my tenacity. I had to find out something was terribly wrong by me insisting that something was wrong and he had to do something. He also asked me to pray for him to the God I served, because it was truly a miracle. He also told me she would be paralyzed, she may have trouble with her speech, and she would be an invalid. I took great confidence in telling him that my Jewish Jesus I have met says she is healed, and that meant HEALED. He also was Jewish. Again, he praised the newfound faith I had and insisted I pray for him, it was my pleasure.

Once more, I was alone with my two babies, no Bill II anywhere. Come to find out, his whole family denied her. What the hell? They denied she was his, how do those devils know? I knew down to the day, time, and sperm, conceived April 25, 1983 on a bet between 12:00 and 1:00 pm PST.

Nevertheless, I pressed on. I found Jesus, and He was powerful, and I wanted to know this gangster who could deliver my sin-sick soul, raise the dead, heal the sick, and deliver me from the demons that had lived and breathed in me. I was done with that, so I thought.

Mama died February 10, 1989. The Lord prepared me for this departure. It was sad for me she had been my number one cheerleader and had become my friend. Mama's last words to me were that she was so sorry she wasn't there for me, that she knew I was being molested, and she didn't know what to do about it, and that if I ever got over what people thought about me I could be anything I set my mind to.

She told me to get the kids out of Los Angeles, to give them a chance. She said her greatest wish for me was that I succeed in Ministry and marry. It was easy to forgive Mama. I had always loved her unconditionally. The only time I'd kept a thought against my mother was when she told me God had cursed her with beauty. I was about twelve years old, and that was the only thing I wanted from God—beauty. I thought every woman wanted that. Was she using drugs because she was beautiful, or because she was weak to the attention men gave her? As I got older, I found out it was the latter, and she had passed the weakness to her eldest daughter. Because of this, I never saw myself as special, no matter how hard I tried. So I struggled with the issue of beauty. Was it a curse or a blessing? This was something I had to find for myself. By saying what she said she robbed and snatched my self-worth, I would pay a high price for this.

She was tired, ready to go, and it was easy and gentle to let her go. There was nothing left unsaid in all her forty-nine years. She had left the cardiologist's office and died in her mother's car, in the back seat. She just leaned over and died.

Mama was insistent that I move out of Los Angeles. I obeyed and moved to North Hollywood, California, to a three bedroom apartment. We began living our lives without Mama, believing we were confident that she had left us with the best she could. I was saved, my relationship with Jesus was strong, and I was assured I had everything I needed to survive and what we didn't have, we would look to God for.

CHAPTER 6
BRYCE, SR

A lady from the block gave me a ride. Without realizing who she was, we drove down to North Hollywood, on Cahuenga Boulevard. She asked me why I didn't remember her. I answered that I didn't.

She replied, "I'm Bryce's sister."

I just looked at her and yelled, "Where is he? I know he's in Texas somewhere, with a bunch of kids!"

She stopped the truck in the middle of the street and told me her brother had been in jail for the past seven years, and nobody had been to see him. She proceeded to tell me the case. She asked, "Do you remember the case when they killed the old white woman on Imperial and Broadway, back in the day?"

When I heard the story all I said in my mind was, *if he's not married, I'm going to get him.* However, I vaguely recalled the case. My mind had been other places, for real, but I remembered that I had dated him for a little while. He would come over to my house and fix Shu and Bill III oatmeal when I was hungover from one of my drug-crazed nights. I also remember his penis was small, but he was nice.

I asked his sister if I could have his mother's number, so I could speak to him. She agreed to take the message.

I talked to his mother, May, about him, a few days later. I waited a week before I could talk to him. He asked me if I was married. Of course, I wasn't, but I had a marriage proposal, and I said, "Yes," *without hesitation*, not wanting to let this get away. I made a deal with God that I would bring him to Christ. I assured Him that my faith was strong, and I could win him, not realizing I'd made a deal with the devil. This decision would try my soul to its core and on the brink of insanity.

I asked him about his stomach, and he asked how I knew that. I explained that the Spirit had showed me five holes in his intestines. I was led to pray for him.

He told me he had Crohn's disease. I didn't quite know what that was, but he explained that his intestines were on fire and they were treating him for it. My thoughts were since my gifts were in operation, I must still be in the will of God. My thoughts would prove me wrong.

He had been in prison for years and no visits.

I picked up in his conversation that his mouth was like a sewer, every other word 'F', 'S', 'MF', 'D', 'HN', 'SOB.' I paused for a moment. I'd read in the Bible that I wasn't supposed to be unevenly yoked with unbelievers, and I felt it was my comfort after losing Mama. I asked him if he believed in Jesus, and of course, he gave me a sincere jailhouse answer.

This was someone I knew; someone I could bring to Jesus. He told me he'd tried to get his brother Johnny to go down the street to get my number, but he told him I had gotten saved, and he was scared. You see, my reputation had spread so big in the hood, nobody had really dealt with me on foolishness; they knew I would be talking Jesus.

I would recognize a demon and send him packing in Jesus name, zeal at its finest. Everyone saw my deterioration, how all over the place my life had gotten, out of control, and *bam,* in one year, I was this on-fire sister for Jesus. I was the Mary Magdalene of the hood. They didn't come for me unless I sent for them.

My family was well known in hood. We gave block parties and house parties, so we had a bit of respect. My brother Monte was a boss, he would teach other young how the cocaine game was operated, a leftover reputation from his Crip days.

We began making plans to get married. I was so afraid someone would tell me not to marry him because he was in prison and that wasn't a good look for my kids.

But I was already committed. When I was praying for him, the Lord told me he was coming home, so I believed God and told him he was, that's where I should have left it!

Well, one person told me not to do it, my cousin Lynn's dad, in Oakland, but I let it roll off' because my mind was made up. Not realizing he had meant well for me, the reason I didn't pay him any mind here's why! In 1978 when I had moved to Oakland, I needed a place to stay, for my son and me. He and his mother had turned me down. At least my great aunt had offered to pay for a room and she was a real witch, I mean a real VODOO WITCH! My four year old son and I slept in my car by a lake, and I remember it like it was yesterday. Someone had been watching us?

Moving on with my plans I was so spooked about the marriage, but I convinced myself it would be all right. At first, they told me we couldn't be married until the next year 1990 but Bryce, Sr. told me we would be married before the year was over, and that's what happened. We were married October 23rd.

One early morning, about 4:30, I had just finished my devotion. I was sitting at my kitchen table, staring outside at the traffic on Magnolia Boulevard, and I heard a still, small voice tell me no. Ignoring this voice, would cost more than I could bear—deception, heartache, humiliation, not realizing I would be opening the door for demon powers to stomp the livin' Lord out of me, to the brink of death, that python demon would choke the very life out of my body if it had not been for ALMIGHTY GOD.

Before I married him, I wanted to go see and talk to him about what had happened, what had landed him to life in prison. A lifer, the word on the street was those niggas ain't never gonna see the streets again. That didn't faze me because I had enough faith for the both of us. He was a brother from the hood who had gotten a bad break. The last time I had talked to Bryce, Sr. he'd said his mom wouldn't sign the contract for him to play for the Globetrotters. He said she didn't trust white people—imagine that. I was told she once belonged to the Nation of Islam, then she joined Jim Jones' church, The Peoples' Temple.

Well, I was approved to go to San Quentin. It was a bit scary; it had such a horrible reputation. So, on the day of the visit, my license had expired, and I was hoping they didn't catch it. I was whispering under my breath, "I hope I get in."

The lady in back of me said, "Don't worry; you will get in."

And I did, so I'm thinking, *cool, God is on my side.* When he came out, he had a sweat attack. I thought it was from seeing someone from the streets for the first time. He came out to the visiting room and ran back in. Now, I think it was because I looked a bit different. I had gained weight, I had Jesus junk, I wasn't a size four anymore. That was a crack size anyway.

We began to talk. He looked a bit different, too. He looked clean. He told me what had happened. He didn't go down the street to hurt the eighty-nine year old lady. When he got down there, the robbery and rape had already taken place. In making an assessment of the situation, he hit the guy in the jaw and broke it, trying to get him off the woman. But the damage was done. The other guy shot her, not before asking Bryce, Sr. to help her, and he said he tried, to no avail. When they came to court in Los Angeles Superior Court, it was overheard that the public defender had said, in a fit of anger, if he had his way, all three of these niggas

would get the death penalty. The two other guys
got twenty-five to life. Bryce, Sr. 15 to life, because
they believed he did try to help the lady and he
came later, while the crime was in progress. The
fifteen to life came when the first jury came back
hung. The jury ask the judge if he could have the
sentence lowered since he came later and tried to
help. After the public defender offered him ten
years, and he declined—dummy—who did this
nigger thing he was, he got fifteen to life and
completed twenty-eight years in prison. "Hind sight
being 20/20." Hmmm?

I, being this noble saint, felt maybe if we
wrote letters, went on a mission to get his
freedom, and garnered support for this man stuck
in this prison who righteously deserved a second
chance, especially now that he would have a wife
and stepchildren, he would get out. I left the prison
feeling like I had a purpose *"Joan of arc"* What a
story of redemption, model prisoner, model family.

Here I was, believing I could fulfill that yearning for a man, and not just any man, a man I knew and felt was safe

We went to the prison on October23rd and got married. My middle son Bill III cried. I wasn't sure why. He might have been intuitive and wanted this madness to stop. He said he was happy for me!

Guess what. The preacher's last name was Murphy. In the hood, that's when someone was running a game on you. Imagine that, unbeknownst to me, I was entering a masterful MURPHY.

We went home which was uneventful and started living our lives. We started making lots of friends in North Hollywood. My kids attended Toluca Lake School. That's when we discovered Bill III had serious talents, truly gifted in dance and music, with a very high IQ.

The first family visit was more about marriage than sex and more than one way to be satisfied! He began to tell about his life and what drove him to the penitentiary. He told how they were members of Jim Jones' church and some of the diabolical things he had seen, while in the red woods. He told me how he planned to be a part of our family and rehabilitate himself. I listened intently, hanging on every word, looking for missteps.

We looked forward to the next family visit. The second time was successful. We were pregnant, and we were happy. He had no other children, and God blessed us with a boy. I didn't like him being a Jr., but he requested, and I granted him that.

It seemed obvious that when Bryce, Sr. went to the Board of Parole, he would give them the letters I had written, and they were good letters, describing how he'd helped the woman and how he had been a model prisoner.

Well, it was 1991 when we sent all the necessary papers to them. I had convinced most of my friends and colleagues that this was a noble cause and he was a good man and they could trust the God me for his freedom. The day came, and he went to the hearing. DENIED! I was crushed. I really thought he would get his freedom. I couldn't talk. I went into a depression for about a week, although I knew I had to get it together for my kids.

We went on with our lives. We blamed Governor Gay Davis for "no prisoner free" politics. We figured we would get them next time. He would call and talk to the kids and give them good advice to live by.

Two years went by uneventful. We moved to Lake View Terrace. It was a beautiful home, and we thought we would be happy there. I decided to go back to school, to better myself. I could give my children something to aspire to. Bill III was very intelligent boy he was intelligent with high academic standards, progressing really fast in the charter school program.

After about four months in the new house, Bryce, Jr. began having night terrors. He couldn't sleep. Every night, his head would be snatched back and forth, like that stuff you see in the Exorcist. Rachel and I prayed and put on gospel music, to ward off the spirits. This happened every night, between 10:30 and 11:00. I would put him in the car, and he would sleep like a baby. Then I knew it was the house. One day, I went to the neighbor's house. He was the person who had showed me the home. I asked him to tell me about the house. He was so distraught as he began to tell me in his broken English about his experience with the property. He said he had gone over to turn on the porch light, and something hit him upside his head. He was so frightened but said nothing. He told me he wanted to tell me when he saw I had small children, but he couldn't. He continued to tell me he believed the prior tenants practiced Santeria, and there were chicken bones around the pool. It's a form of witchcraft, primarily practiced in Latin culture.

Every Wednesday, an owl would sit in the tree, facing the pool. Well, I didn't need to hear any more. I knew the house was possessed, and they didn't want us there. I was sure my tongues frustrated them but not enough to make them leave. I wondered why I didn't have enough power to send them from the house.

Well, one day at Phillips College, I asked one of my prayer partners and class mates about this entity.

She quickly replied, "Where is the open door? There's a breach somewhere, and he has a way in." and they were there before you were and they intend to stay? And I didn't have enough power to exercise them out?

I knew for the first time I had let this devil in by my disobedience, and my family would be under attack.

Bill III came to me and said the Lord told him we had to move or Bryce, Jr. would never have any peace. He was twelve years old.

We enlisted help to aid with these demons tormenting Bryce, Jr.. My spiritual mother came and did an exorcism; it lasted about a week. Two weeks later, the Lord blessed us with $2200.00, and we moved to Fontana. When Bryce Sr. called, he told me before I could tell him, we would be moving to Fontana. Hmm, what spirit is working here? He wasn't saved. I accepted him as the head of our family, I believe the man is the head, I felt I could sanctify the husband through a sanctified wife.

We had a beautiful condo and good schools when we left the haunted house. I graduated from college. I had a degree in my hand, and I had earned it. My secret reason I went back to school was to hear *Pomp and Circumstance*, I ask the dean of the school if I made a 4.0 GPA would he let me have 3 minutes to speak he enthusiastically said yes, and that I did and received a spot to speak as an honorary Valedictorian, with my kids there to see it.

Soon, another parole board hearing was coming around. This time, I told my husband I couldn't deal with the swearing, and if he couldn't communicate with me, then we couldn't talk. The phone bills were high, and I was not paying for the filthy language. He got the message, and we sent another round of support letters. Again, the request was denied. Once again, I went into a funk, but this time, I gave him a year's break.

I had met a guy name Mark. He was not very nice-looking, but his body was what a woman dreamed of. He worked as an oil engineer. We talked of getting married quite a bit. He was concerned about my kids going to college and he felt I should be planning for their future and they didn't need a stepdaddy who was in prison. We went all sorts of places, and we had fun. Well, I sincerely thought about divorce. Here's what stopped it—I sought counsel, because I believed there was safety in sound counsel. I was advised that I should see the victory through.

Then our neighbor, who was crazy about Bryce, Jr., came up one day as I sat outside reading my Bible and said, "God told me to tell you not to divorce your husband." Now, these were some pretty respectable people in The Foursquare Church—*the church Amie Semple McPherson started*—and they were white and very established, so the word of knowledge made me pay close attention.

I listened to the advice they gave me and stayed. We joined their organization and stayed for seven years, in Riverside, California. My kids were growing beautifully. We had everything we needed, a beautiful ministry, faithful friends, and solid family members. I certainly had my village, and I took full advantage of my resources.

Bryce, Sr. would tell me when a blessing was coming, and sure enough, it would come. He wrote spiritual letters, and they began to be impressive, although I knew he had help. I knew he had the education level of a ninth grader, but that didn't matter because I knew determination with a plan was powerful. He had begun to embrace this powerful man called Jesus.

Another date would come for his hearing and, again, DENIED.

By now, we had moved to Pinyon Avenue in Fontana we had a beautiful home theater with a swimming pool and 7 fruit trees, we a lot of parties there as well I had a good job, working for Riverside County in the Black Infant Program. We all worked this program like our lives depended on it. We also won several awards for the work we accomplished. Once in my cubicle, I was praying for my Cocker Spaniel dog whose name was my Midget—(*guess where I got name*)—to come home. He had been missing for two weeks, and I was praying in a soft whisper.

My co-worker leaned over the cubicle and said, "What dog are you praying for?" I knew the gossip was thick; I had never kept it a secret. I was a faith believer. Come to find out, her dude was in the Federal Penitentiary, imagine that! I know they thought I was a damn fool, acting like Joan of Arc again " I am woman, hear me roar."

The years were passing, and things were starting to get serious for Bill III. We started looking into college, after he graduated with a 4.5. He was smart and good looking his future was bright.

We had addressed his homosexuality many times. Of course, I was concerned about him. We were devout Christians, and the Bible was clear. However, in hind sight, I should have approached this subject very differently. My job was to teach him to be God-fearing, law abiding, and a good citizen and trust he could figure the rest out on his own. When Bill III and I ran into problems with his life, I got on my knees and apologized for being dogmatic about his choice. I should have approached it with love and compassion, the same way I approached everyone else. It was his life, his choice. Today, Bill III is one of the fiercest promoters for GOAG, as well as my other two sons.

I sent packages every three months to Bryce, Sr., even sacrificing to make sure he had everything he needed. I thought it was teaching my children that helping others in need was a way of life for us. At times, there were days I could see the damage it was doing to my children, having them subjected to murmurings and whispers.

Nevertheless, we forged ahead and believed God would bring him home soon. We got Bill III into college, first, junior college and then, to UCLA. It was my greatest hope for him to finish. He had received a scholarship to Virginia Tech for Drill Instruction. I didn't quite see it that way. I wanted him closer to home. Again, looking back, it was probably the wrong decision, keeping him in California.

The prison became a burden too big to bear, the visits, the phone calls, the packages. I started feeling the burden financially. He didn't seem to care about that; he felt he had a partner who could handle everything. After all, I'd had been with gangbanger boyfriends, snitch boyfriends, gangster sugar daddy companions, all of whom made being married to a lifer a seen like a breeze, with the most exceptional relationship of all was JESUS.

The Holy Spirit told me he was coming home. I preached a message from the scripture, Luke 18, about the woman who went to the unjust judge, to avenge her of her adversary. It said thou he neither feared God nor regarded man, because she troubled him, he will avenge her. *Because she troubled him!* Though she cries LONG; how long will she have to wait? NOT LONG!! NOT LONG!! I made myself feel better about my journey.

We were approaching denial number five from The Board of Parole. I still questioned if he'd told me what really happened, or had he glammed it up for me? In the parole hearing, they asked him if his wife was an attorney. Wow, that was an impressive comment. However, it was still denied!

I was following all the news coverage about what was going on, reading up on everything pertaining to parole and prisoners I did recognize the wave of reform in the prison system but it was a long time coming! There was so much overcrowding in the jails.

When they took our family visits away but gave them to the gays, I thought what the hell? This would surely lead to adultery. The family visits were created for the lifers, in an effort to keep their families together.

***

Bryce, Jr. had been complaining of lower stomach pain. Rachel called me at work to inform me she thought it was serious and I needed to come home. I instructed her to give him half of one of my Darvocet, to help stop the pain, to no avail.

I scurried home to see what was wrong he was worse than I thought; we had to take him to San Bernardino Hospital. When we finally arrived, they examined him and gave him some Vicodin and antibiotics. This was before the epidemic of pain pills, but we who had prescriptions got our meds all the time. Well, we didn't accept the diagnosis. He looked like he was in serious pain.

Rachel was fuming. She YELLED at the doctors, "If you don't find out what's wrong with my brother, Ima pull a John Q up in here."

Surely, it must have put the fear of God in them, as they ordered a helicopter to take him to Loma Linda, although we decided to take him ourselves. When we arrived at the hospital, they took him in right away. Hours soon became days.

Dr Kno grilled me about what medication I had given him for the pain, too. Snap! I didn't want to fess up I certainly knew it was a controlled substance. He said he already knew, but he wanted me to tell him, and he assured me that was the end. He had to put him on Morphine for the level of pain he was in. Then, what the hell? They informed us he had the pancreas of a ninety year old man he was only an 11 year boy, Well, I didn't drink, but my neighbor did, where Bryce, Jr. had spent a lot of time with his boys. He came to the hospital, to assure me in a panic that he had never given Bryce, Jr. any beer. I knew that already. He had five boys whom I loved dearly. Weeks were going by. They switched the Morphine to Demerol. On about the fortieth day in the hospital, my son told me he liked the feeling of the medicine. My heart sank, that statement coming from a child with a long line of substance abuse family members mother and father, He was only 11 years old. He'd spent fifty-one days in the hospital and on drugs. I feared for his future, but I put it in prayer. His sister was the wisdom here. Don't mess with Rachel! She pressed the issue and made the hospital find the problem.

***

Two years had passed. I moved from Fontana in 2006, to Colton, California. Bryce, Jr. had started acting up. I was really frustrated, so to make myself happy, I purchased a black on silver Jaguar for myself. I drove it everywhere. No matter what situation I found myself in, I kept myself a nice ride. Bryce, Jr. was acting out in school, fighting, disrupting the classroom. When we confronted him, he claimed it was because he had left his other high school, in Fontana.

I will say this, Bill III and Rachel left a record that was hard to live up to at Fontana High School I received parent of the year many times. I would get a sense of dread every time I received these awards, because I knew this would be tested. But I enjoyed seeing them progress. Rachel and Bill III were two of easiest children to raise, until they reached eighteen. Then, *bam*, they left the church, left the house, and I hardly recognized them.

Bryce, Jr. was out of control. We had him in basketball, and he was quite good. His team had won the semi-finals, to go to the finals. Bryce, Jr. being the tallest on the team, was essential to winning the championship. Well, he got caught stealing, and we had to settle on a punishment. In a phone conversation with his jailhouse father, he told me NOT to let him play under any circumstances. I had always given him that authority. After all, we were a family. Well, the coach came and pleaded that we find another punishment because they needed Bryce, Jr. to win. I turned him down, then the team came and begged me. I knew I was going against his father, but I let him play—the second greatest mistake I ever made. When his father found out, he was furious. The conversation went something like this. "By you letting him play, and they lost, he learned he was not that necessary. If they had won, and he not played, he would have respect for the other teammates, but you jacked up his responsibility to his actions."

It was the only advice he gave that I thought was genuine. From that point on, my son had no respect for my discipline, and it would be to his disadvantage.

One evening in November 2006, while watching television, there a knock on my door. It was the police, so I kindly asked them what I could do for them. They asked me if my name was Mrs. West, and of course, I replied that it was. Then, they asked if I had a son named Bryce West, Jr.. I thought someone was hurt, so I drove down the street, where the other policemen were, but I stayed calm. I saw Bryce, Jr. in the police car. When the officer told me what happened, I couldn't believe it! Here's how the story goes.

The two of them, Ronnie and Bryce, broke into a white woman's apartment, to steal her belongings. The woman came home and caught them in action. Ronnie escaped out the window. The woman yelled at Bryce, Jr. and told him to *sit down*. Imagine that; she gave a mother's command. Well, Ronnie came down the street, to tell the police it was his idea. I couldn't believe this. It was the very same way his father got caught up, in 1982, Now, his son was well on his way to becoming an accessory after the fact, which carried the same jail time, especially if you were a black teen. It *was* accessory; he had gotten caught in the house.

To add insult to injury, his public defender said he could get him off. He asked me if Bryce, Jr. was slow, if he had ADHD.

Bryce, Jr. yelled out, "I ain't slow!"

So, he quickly said, "I can't help him, because he will sabotage his own case." It was too late; he would have a record. I was glad he got caught and didn't get shot, because that is what you call a righteous kill.

It was Thanksgiving 2007, and my stress level was high, meaning my blood pressure was out of control.

I decided to move him out of California to Texas. I really didn't know anyone who lived in Texas, but Bryce, Jr. had aunts and cousins there; maybe they could help me with him and have some positive influence on him. WRONG!! He smoked more weed in Texas than he did at home.

On March 31st, I picked him up at his cousin's house. He was so high, if I touched him, he would fall over. That day, I told him I was leaving the next day. I was completely done with this. I had given up my job and my home, and he still didn't want to change his trifling ways. It didn't matter to him that I was constantly making sacrifices to give him a better chance. Even though he didn't appreciate basketball, it would have helped put some fundamentals in place for his adult life, and it would have helped him get a scholarship for college.

I really had nowhere to go, but it was home. His aunt told me she would give me a place to stay! The witch treated me like I was a piece of "S" and actually turned my son against me. I had never seen demons like these. My niece and her husband let me stay with them until I found my place in Arlington, Texas.

I was so humiliated; this was one ungrateful child. I left Texas April 1st. I was on the road, but I knew my welcome was growing thin, so I did it— movin'. I sure won't mess with Texas again. This attitude would be the same attitude I would face with his father shortly, on a demonic scale that would only take God to deliver me, and the cold truth is I had exposed my family to monumental drama.

I went back to California. My daughter Rachel took me in until I could figure out what I wanted to do. I needed to think. I would be with my granddaughters, and that was the joy of my life to be with them again pure agape love. We moved to the Rialto Estates. This was a nice community, with a swimming pool, fireplace, and beautiful gardens. Before I agreed to move to this house, I told Rachel I didn't want to move with her baby daddy. They weren't married, and it was my money that would pay for it. So we planned a garden wedding at the new house.

One morning, I was watching cartoons, and I don't even like cartoons. In my backyard, was the deputy sheriff, asking me to come to the front. I asked him what was he doing in my backyard. He said for me to come outside. When I walked around to the front, I saw Bryce, Jr. in handcuffs. Here we go again!

The officer pulled me to the side and said these words, "He had a rifle and was pointing it at cars as they passed. A UPS driver called the police and told them it was a young black male. The captain out of the Fontana unit told me he had his sharp-shooter ready, across the street, he was ready to 'SHOOT TO KILL', but in one moment, the sharp-shooter said he heard a voice tell him to STOP! **He didn't know what he was doing**, and the officer made commands for him to get on the ground. He complied, needless to say. I went numb all over. The captain commented that I must be a praying mother. Yes, I was, but I couldn't tell how it was working, how he didn't realize that him pointing a GUN at strangers was another righteous kill. The captain told me to take him in the garage and whoop his ass, and they would stand watch until it was done. And I couldn't. I was hitting at the air, no power, no strength. He was throwing his precious life away. The guilt I felt was real. I asked him what he was struggling with, and he told me he didn't like being born to a father in prison. The truth, to my shame, and the dagger pierced! I told him Jesus was born in a manger! *a barn*

I was done. I gave him all the money I had and told him wherever he wanted to go, I would send him, but I couldn't take the drama. I gave all I had and took him to the bus. Emotionally and physically, I was on the verge of a stroke and a heart attack and a nervous breakdown, He went back to Texas, but I was done, and I would pray for him.

I resolved in my heart that I had done all I could to help him. I needed a real change; my surroundings were closing in on me. This child had run my patience in the ground. He had no regard for the sacrifices we had made for him. His brother Shu had always made sure he had what he needed to be in sports. When he started smoking weed, it took over his life. He was already lazy, and weed made him worse.

I decided to go to Arizona, to stay a while with my beloved sister, Denise, who had bought a beautiful home in Maricopa. She took mercy on me; due to the fact I was at my wits' end.

I learned my way around Arizona fast, met lots of people, and made some friends. I was amazed at how beautiful the sunsets were. I got various little jobs to make some cash. I got hired at a research company. It paid well, and I was able to maintain my Jaguar and go to all the cool places in the city. Denise wouldn't take any cash. She just wanted me to recover. I was in full-blown menopause, with real heartaches and total depression, from prison issues. I was going down fast. God needed to intervene, and He needed to do it fast.

I decided to focus on "me." I lost forty pounds, not even trying. I think it was the weather, and I looked good. One day, I was gassing up the car, and a gentleman watched me go across the walkway. I felt his eyes on me in admiration. For the second time in my life, I felt like a star. I just held my head up and strutted across, like I was on display.

***

It wasn't working out in Texas for Bryce, Jr. He starting feeling the pressure of taking care of himself, so he begged me to ask his auntie if he could come and stay. I thought about it for a while and decided to have mercy. After all, God is merciful to me. So, I asked his auntie Denise, and she gave him two rules: first, he would have to go to school and maintain his grades, and second, he could not bring that drama to her house. He agreed and came to stay with us.

It was time for another board hearing for Bryce, Sr. It was 2009, and this was the eighth try at getting his freedom. I had put a proposal together with one hundred taxpayers' signatures and addressed it to The Governor of the State of California, Arnold Schwarzenegger, and to the Board of Parole. It was late in the evening, about 8:00, when I got the call that they had approved his release. I was walking out of the tub and fell to the floor, praising God.

Everything had come to fruition, and finally, we had gotten the victory! I talked to Bryce, Sr. for a minute on the phone, and after twenty eight years' incarceration, he was coming home, to us, to a family who had loved and cared for him every step of the way.

We all had sacrificed so much for him and truly loved him. We waited, with anticipation and joy, to finally be together as a family, to start sharing and making memories for our forever folder.

Since I lived in Arizona, it was going to be a challenge for us. He arrived home the day before Thanksgiving. My sister offered for him to come to

Arizona. That didn't pan out, so Bryce, Jr. and I headed to California.

CHAPTER 7

THE Revealing of the Betrayal

When I talked to him on the first day, I got an inkling or hint. He said something like, "I'll catch you later." I ignored the strange words and chalked it up to the fact he wasn't used to being free. The plan was to meet at his brother's house in Los Angeles.

So we arrived, and when Bryce, Jr. hugged his father, it truly was something special. After years of waiting, to see his father a free man was a blessing. He cried as if he was waiting to let go of all the anxiety and anger he finally made peace with, he had to be free from his troubles in his own mind. We all sat around and talked and tried to remember the good ol' days, but it was time to get down to business. Bryce, Sr. and I made love for the first time in seven years. We went to the Marriott hotel on Century Boulevard.

My brother- in-law offered for us to stay at their house. It was the size of a dollhouse, but we took it. We felt so blissful, it didn't matter.

I went to Rachel's, in Riverside, to make her some gumbo, which is to die for, for the New Year. When I went back, I thought I'd dress up and surprise Bryce, Sr., but the response I got was, "You smell like gumbo!"

Damn, that's all I got, after I took pleasure in getting fancy for him.

We were headed into a New Year, 2010. New Year's Eve night, we went to a dance with his folks. It was nice; we danced and had some champagne.

While praying about our situation, I was led back to Arizona, with my sister Denise, and I left him the jaguar, at first I questioned it because he didn't have a driver's license. We kept getting into spats and arguments, but we were getting to know each other's ways. To tell the truth, we didn't get along, but we were married, and I had labored for twenty-one years for this to work.

Shu gave Bryce, Sr. $1000.00, to buy himself some clothes. I went back to Arizona with Denise, but before I left, my sister-in-law sat down with me and had a real woman-to-woman talk.

She said, "Are you sure you want to leave him right now? These women are going to devour him, with him fresh out of prison, clean, and looking nice."

I told her, "I have to be obedient to the Lord."

She straight up and told me she didn't know why the Lord would say that, and I understood she didn't quite get my conviction.

Then she said, "Well, you did say he was coming home, so I guess you have to do what you gotta do, sis."

When Bryce, Sr. and I talked before I left, he asked me if I was really going to leave him. But all through his being in prison, I thought I was following the lead of The Holy Spirit, so he accepted it. I left him the car and went to Arizona. We talked every day, on the phone. It was strange, at first, not hearing the recording say, 'This call is from a correctional institution.'

We looked forward to seeing other. I went back and forth, from Arizona to Los Angeles, in the truck my sister gave me. This went on for about two months. When I went back one weekend, to take him the truck and pick up my Jaguar, I found kids' clothes in my backseat. I tried to think of children in the family, and I just left it alone. . All hell hit the fan, when my cousin from Main Street Crips called me and said she'd seen some woman driving my car. She asked me if I wanted her to take of it, this was major no-no in the hood, my cousin was no joke!!

While I was back in Arizona I got a call that he was in the hospital. When I talked to him, he didn't want me to come to LA. Of course, I thought this was a bit strange, but I didn't go. About three weeks later, I surprised him. He was furious, but I began to suspect the devil was in the game, and my attitude changed to suspicious.

This was major no-no in the hood, so I went to California to address this issue. Denial, denial, denial, he swore it wasn't my car they saw, that he wouldn't let another woman drive my car. I wanted to believe him, for my sake. I didn't like the emotions I was feeling, so I did everything to suppress them, even if I had to be a big girl and give him time to get his curiosity out and realize he had a family who had spent part of a lifetime supporting him.

We starting going to church. There was a church in the hood called the Reckin Crew that was a former gangbanger's church, and he was very powerful in Deliverance Ministry. We decided to visit one Sunday. At the end of the service, the bishop had an altar call, so I got in the line.

Whatever the Lord had to say, I was ready to hear. He declared that God would give me double portions of anointing. I didn't know exactly what he meant. That God was going to show me what it was I was called to do? I had been in women's ministry for some time. The prophesy was a bit unclear, but I've learned to let God reveal it in its due seasons. So he got up and got into the line! He told him that he'd made a covenant with God for his freedom, that God will call that promise on his life , he made a promise he never meant to keep Oh, boy!!! That was all I needed to hear. I knew then, I was in trouble, and everything I was hoping and praying for had been a deception.

He wanted my relationship with Jesus to sustain his release and be his runner. I couldn't believe what I was hearing. God relieving his MOTIVES, who could argue with that? I had been masterfully played. I tried to believe it was something different. How could I defend this? It was from a preacher who wasn't involved in our relationship. I lost a piece of myself that day, and as the days went on, I would lose much, much more.

I was in for a battle I didn't know how to fight. My life had been raising my children, church ministry, getting my husband his freedom our freedom.

All of my suspicions had been magnified, everything the people in the hood said he was doing in our neighborhood flaunting his adultery for the world to see. I was so humiliated, and with a heartache that was so deep, I cannot put it into words. I would come to town, and he wouldn't be where he said he'd be. He would tell me lies on top of lies, the deception coming so fast, I couldn't keep up. He was a different person than I knew. I was watching this person, who I believed was worthy of my love that I freely gave him.

I continued to go to church and tried to be normal as possible. Then one day, I left church to meet Bryce, Sr. to have a conversation, but this conversation wouldn't be what I wanted to hear. He told me to let him go. I was devastated. I told him he had to be out of his mind; I didn't sacrifice twenty-one years of my life to let this be over in a year. I gave him my family, my friends, and my church family. They all believed in him and prayed for him, and he had disregarded all that they had done. And furthermore, he had treated our sacrifice like a piece of crap. I was not in this conversation. I really couldn't comprehend what was going down. I was thinking about how was I going to do damage to this fool who had used me to the fullest extent, and I wasn't in a forgiving mood. I had murder on my mind and contemplating how I was going to do it.

He swore he didn't mean for things to turn out like this. Everyone was in complete devastation, because they all believed in him and the marriage. The word on the street was he'd disrespected the game; he'd left me out in the cold and didn't give a damn. The one thing he was supposed to be was loyal to the one who had stayed down with him for twenty-one years. Even the streets rejected him and tried to make him see how far out of line he was and how he'd made the wife of a lifer seem like crap.

One day at church, I was on the pulpit, and I was a complete mess. I had let so many unclean spirits in my flesh, they had begun to manifest. I was begging him to have sex with me, just to be close, to just to hear his voice. One night in his truck, we were having sex, and he said he was ashamed of himself. He was sneaking around to have sex with his wife, although his cock seemed bigger, or maybe I just wanted sex that bad, or I just wanted my husband back. My pastor confronted me about what he saw in my spirit. He reminded me the demons come back seven times stronger than when they left. Although he knew my current journey was fire, I had a responsibility to the women's ministry, and I needed to check myself and do it fast.

It was my friend, Bell Rickes, who helped me through this diabolical maze I was in. Bell was a lady I had grown up knowing, on 105th Street. Everyone called her a witch. She didn't let her kids play with us, and she really didn't socialize with us. I met her one day, when I was working to getting signatures for certain initiatives on the ballot. I approached her to sign one.

Her response was, "I don't sign no G-dam papers, because I don't vote." She invited me in for coffee, and that coffee turned into seven years. Our relationship will go down in history. I told her all the things I was going through. Of course, she thought I was a damn fool, but she was gracious. She also saw how it was tearing my fiber of my soul apart. She became as close as me as my mother. She told me she had five bottles of Norco pain pills, for one dollar a piece, and if I knew someone who could use them, I could have a bottle free.

Needless to say, I knew a lot of people who needed them, including me. Bell and I grew closer every day. She welcomed me in her home. I could spend the night at her house, use her car, borrow money, but you can bet, she wanted it back. She was gangster about her paper.

One summer night, Lavell and I were sitting on the porch, drinking tequila shots. Bryce, Sr. had moved in with his girlfriend. I decided to call him and tell him we needed to get the divorce. My family saw this marriage was making me lose reality. It just hurt so bad, so much shame. I didn't know what to do when that reproach fell on me like bricks on my head. Well, I told him he would pay half of the divorce and no one's money is going to touch it. My sisters and my son Shu had done enough.

I had been drinking tequila with Bell, and something was in the air when he answered. He told me, "What do you want? I am with my woman.

Oh, snap! I got in Shu's 750 silver Benz and drove the four blocks it took me to get there, knocked on the door, and his girlfriend answered. I asked for my husband, and she told me I was disturbing her house.

He came out with fire in his eyes, not considering the fire in mine. We took the argument to the street, which was Main Street. Before I knew it, she came up behind and hit me in the jaw. I looked at her French braids and went into gangster mode. I tied her hair in my fingers and beat her ass. I slammed her on the ground. Something came over me, and I lost control. Twenty-one years of sacrifice, and I'm disrupting her household? He finally pulled me off her. Her friends were rooting for her to whip my old ass. Too late. I'm ten years older than she is, but I guess she didn't know who she was hittin'! The last fight I had; I was thirteen.

Bell called me about ten times. She said she went to get her deed, because she knew she might have to bail me out of jail. I sat in the car until 5:00 that morning, crying, trying to figure out how it had come to this, how was I so deceived—from the hood, been with gangbangers, balers, and gangsters, a woman of God, and a college graduate—so naïve, so stupid.

I knew the Holy Spirit wasn't pleased with this situation. Neither was I; my heart was tearing, like it was disposable tissue, and I was lost. I had let myself down. I had let God down. I had let my family down as well. But I wondered where that burst of strength came from. Where we grew up, if someone hit you, you hit back and let them feel that disrespect, and make them feel you   she disrespected me ,she got what she was looking for. Period.

Well, Rachel heard about the fight and was ready to defend my honor. No matter how bad we were getting along, she had my back. This brought more attention to everything this   unwanted attention. Shu had purposed in his heart, he was going to kill Bryce, Sr., not even considering he was his brother's father. You see, he's a Main Street Mafia member, and they are dead serious about violations, but this violated my honor, my soul, and my mind. I wasn't functioning like a minister; I was functioning like a woman, a defeated woman. I lost myself in the dissolving of this marriage.

My cousin Carrie died, and we gave her a block party to celebrate her home going. Bryce, Sr. came, and my elder cousin Marcy told him to get his "MF" ass off her property and not to come back. "If it wasn't for Gail, you wouldn't even be free." She was the first one to see him with his girlfriend on Century Blvd she said she started to run them over but decided against it, as she was eighty-five years old. We all were standing outside by some trash cans that were set up for the party.

Shu fixed his eyes on Bryce, Sr. and readied himself to do him harm.

I saw the look in his eyes and told him, "He's not worth it, son! He's not worth it!" I was scared for Shu. I had brought this man into our lives, and he wasn't worth what we put into his life. In the Spirit, I saw Bryce, Sr. falling over the trash cans and those Crohns bursting, and him losing his life, and my son going to prison, for what I had brought into their lives. I saw when the Spirit touched his heart and he backed off. I thank God he did that.

I knew I had to put an end to this marriage and maybe somehow free myself from this misery that had been unleashed. So I went to the Compton courthouse and filed the necessary papers.

I woke up early one morning and was praying that I get free from the unclean spirit that I had allowed to enter my soul. He was in adultery, was in fornication, all those unclean spirits came in my spirit, and I knew it. The word was also reveling my sin as well as my prayers, and my prayers were simply, "Deliver me out of this hell I am in." it was more than I could bear. I was at six to seven Norcos a day, to kill the pain I was feeling inside, but it was temporary. I believe the Lord let me feel the pain he felt when I broke his heart, when I disobeyed that still small voice, at a time when, if I would have just obeyed, my life would have been a lot different.

While making peace with God and myself, there was a lot of work to do, and I knew I had to do the work. As Iyanla Vanzant says, "You got to do the work." I do agree with that part!

In November, while vacuuming, the following thing happened to me. I heard the Holy Spirit say, "Your husband is in the hospital."

I immediately sat down, answered back, and said, "What do you want me to do with that information?"

I didn't get an answer, but I was preparing to go to Lala's house—my middle sister—to pick up some cash and visit my Grandmother "Madear" Cochran in the convalescent hospital, which is across from the hospital where Bryce, Sr. was, so I planned three trips.

I arrived at the hospital on the second stop. I went up to his room, and he was livid, mad as hell.

He said, "Who told you I was here?"

I told him, "You know who told me. He hasn't stopped talking to me just because you have."

The doctor came in the room then, and he introduced me to her as his wife Of course, she looked at me and probably knew I wasn't the woman who had been visiting him. She took off her gloves and gave me a handshake of respect. I guess I didn't look like the chicken head he'd been with.

He got into his wheelchair and hurried like he was going to get busted or something for being with his wife! we found a place outside in the garden. Wow in a garden where all the damage originally started, but this time it was Adam!!! That was deceived by satan.

I bent down and told him, "I hope it was worth it. I feel like I am grieving a dead man. I have accepted the fact that I was used as a conduit to freedom. I accept the fact I was just a runner for a stranger. I accept that you didn't care for me. I *don't* accept the fact that you hurt and betrayed my kids and made it hard for them to trust people and believe in them. You have set the example for our son that may haunt him the rest of his life. God have mercy on you for that." I turned and walked away.

Immediately, I heard the Holy Spirit say, "Don't look back."

And I didn't. I was drenched. I felt like I had lost five pounds. I was free spiritually, and it was manifested in my flesh. When I was backing out, I saw him in my rearview mirror.

He rolled up on the side and said, "I don't even know what I am doing, myself."

I told him, "That's the smartest thing you've said since you left the penitentiary."

I drove off; I still had my grandmother to visit. She perceived something serious was going on, and I told her everything. She only had one sentence for me. "Don't let it be anybody's decision to divorce but yours." Then she told me she wanted some food.

Bryce, Sr. was burning my phone up, but I didn't answer while I was with my grandmother. When I left her, I picked up the phone, and for the first time, I heard what was to sound like an apology. I listened but told him to catch me on a flyer. I have no idea why I said that, but I said it and hung up.

It was over. I felt the bond break that day. I knew God had released me from this marriage, although the pain and humiliation was there and I would have to walk this out every day, one minute at a time, one hour, until it reached twenty-four, and then start over again. I would push ahead, with the help of my sisters and sons and daughter and LaBell. I knew I could do this. I had communities and cities rooting for me, to overcome this onslaught of evil I had endured

When I left all three stops that day, I was so exhausted and drained emotionally it was hard to feel anything but shame and humiliation, I took the 110 FWY. Waiting for the evening before I headed back to Rachel's house in San Bernardino I received a call from one of my dearest friends who lives in Moreno Valley California, she asked me if I wanted to go to a gospel talent show at the Staples Center in downtown Los Angeles, I didn't want to talk to anyone, I was trying to figure out how to think and how to feel. I tried unsuccessfully to get out of going, well I relented and went. Parking was $10 dollars, I had $10.00 to my name.

When I arrived at arena, I saw a member of the early church where I attended, I was feeling self-conscious. I was sure she saw the pain on my face. well we were seated, we couldn't sit together as I sat listing to Mary Mary grade the gospel choirs, I realize my mind was being locked, I couldn't quite understand what was going on I had never had this experience before. Suddenly a voice WHEN YOU WERE WITH MS E ON YOUR WAY TO HER SON'S HOUSE... I HAVE GIVEN YOU THAT MINISTRY...GIRLFIREND OF A GANGBANGER, BLOOD CRIES FROM THE GRAVE..MANY ARE HURTING AND NEED DELERVENCE...I WILL ANSWER...MILLIONS WILL FEEL MY POWER AND I WILL POUR OUT MY SPIRIT...SALVATION WILL ARISE IN THEIR HEARTS. And many other things I heard that day that I keep in my heart and ponder them. I tried to respond to tell Jesus I didn't like the name,

I was a glamour girl I liked wigs, eyelashes, make up and fancy clothes. But to no avail. When he had released me from this trance, I knew beyond a shadow of a doubt I had went to the Staples Center so God could speak to me and I'm so glad today that I didn't look back perhaps I would have turned into a pillar of salt and tried to make that marriage work, my testimony today is " GOD I LISTENED." GOAGINC would be my saving grace, Proverbs 29:18 declares WITHOUT A VISION THE PEOPLE PERISH', imagine working in ministries all those years faithfully. A faithful God gave me my own vineyard to work, and work it has been, every day the lord adds to GOAGINC. As he wills We have a faithful American and International following . GOAGINC is not a church where we gather, we are a witnessing ministry arm of the body of Jesus Christ. We have associates.

La Bell sat me down one day and told me she hoped she had been to me what my mother would have been if she were here. That was the most precious thing the "witch" could have said to me, when I was so broken in spirit. I told her I knew that her assignment, at the time, was to get me on my feet to do ministry again. She did that, and she was my angel, because she did what was necessary and said what was necessary, to get me thinking. Not on myself so much, but on how to move on. She gave me personal lessons on how to handle men, and she had been a pro. And she wasn't even a Christian yet. When she died in 2019, I went her homegoing service and cried like a baby.

Epilogue

The Healing

"The Balm in Gilead"

This story was written for my healing and deliverance. I have written these words in blood, and I have opened myself up to massive vulnerability. But I have been prepared for this journey all my life. It is very clear to me that my choices have been the catalyst for my pain and suffering. However, I feel if I'd had better parenting, perhaps I would have looked at the world differently.

Due to the fact that I was molested young, it influenced some of my decisions. As for my father Sam, I believe God knew exactly where he wanted me to be placed. When Sam died in 2016, he repented on his deathbed. He shared with me that he regretted the things he had not contributed to my life. He spoke of what he thought would be my legacy. I would give almost anything to have heard that blessing in my life when I needed it.

One thing he did say, was that I had the ability to have whatever I wanted, but I was scared of myself. That literally was only thing he said that didn't sound like I was trifling, which he liked to remind me of. In the end, I could very well tell him where I got my trifling from. I am sure, on his deathbed, he had to know he had a role in this behavior.

His penis had swollen to an unbelievable size, and he feared his immortality. I made a deal with him before he died. I could see the fear in his eyes. I said to him, 'You don't have to fear death, if you know Jesus. If you accept Jesus Christ, we are on the same ground. I won't fear life and never lose my confidence to get on my journey to live. With Jesus, you won't fear death because we all must face death."

He immediately said, "I will take that bet." Him being a true betting man, I was sure he would keep his end of the deal. Unfortunately, he died a few days later, so it would be up to me to keep mine. When he died, I hadn't come into my full deliverance. It wasn't until 2017, when, one night, I heard Sam's voice call me out of slipping into death. God used a voice I was familiar with, and I listened. So I guess Sam did play a role in me being Born Again, for the third time. I made my peace with Sam, even though he had given me words I couldn't use, but I found out I *can* use them, because he knew who I was and my potential, and finally, I believe it.

Raymond Washington, the Crip leader, did give me some good advice and tried to make sure I knew how important I should have been to myself. Although his words had little effect, they were true, and they came from a genuine place in his soul.

I recall the last conversation I had with him, on my mother's back porch on the block, and I quote, 'I'm not going to live long, because the powers that be want me to start up gang violence on a whole different level, so Tom Bradley don't get the Mayor's office.' I really couldn't comprehend at the time what he was trying to tell me. Two weeks later, he was dead. The word on the street is he slapped a friend of his girlfriend's, and that was the death sentence. I learned of his children, when I started GOAG, and I have had the pleasure of meeting his daughter. Whatever the truth is, he died.

D-Bob, I didn't see myself for seeing him. Most of my education came from this relationship, but I lost that in drugs. He and Mama became good friends, and he and his son are good friends today. He and Shu are homeowners. He is one of the few Q102 Crips that is still alive.

I can see him today, and it's like two ships passing in the night. The best thing that happened in that relationship is my beautiful boy, who is the only child I call FRIEND. I'm often accused of having a favorite child, but the truth is I committed more sins in Shu's presence and did many unspeakable things around him than the other three, and I get the most respect from this child. One thing he saw is I respected and loved my mother. We took her to the Tarzana Methadone Clinic appointment five days a week, for a year.

All the sex I felt was so good, wasn't so good for me. All this was a form of rebellion from my father and stepfather's abuse; it was a way to escape for me. I felt like I was getting something that felt good to me, knowing all along, I was being played. But I did learn I had a backbone. When he crossed that bridge, he lost me, and that was that. I finally stood for something, and that something was ME!

Mr. Green was a different story. He was meeting my drug and financial needs, only to systematically lose my self-respect, not realizing the enormous toll it would play on my psyche, especially how this tore down my will to believe in myself. It's a form of laziness. You are always looking for someone else to provide for you, and it gives you a false since of entitlement.

When I entrusted the son, Lloyd Jr., to my bosom and bed, I was literally in the throes of witchcraft, and I knew it. No matter how I convinced myself I was in love with him and despised his father, I have no illusion on how I could have saved him. Knowing that I could not stop fate nor could I have brought anything healthy to the relationship, realizing that what I was feeling inside, I brought on myself. In searching my soul, I knew it would take God to help me feel like I was worth loving again and to feel like a worthwhile woman.

Well, all I can say is Billy Jean is not my lover. A time of life lessons, a time of selfishness, what I saw in the graveyard, I should have left there. Brains beat beauty every time! My cousin J

Bo tried to warn me that was a song I didn't want

to sing. Some of my greatest trials would come

through this encounter, however, also some of my

greatest joys. When I write my conclusions to these

relationships, they may seem small. It's because

they are. When Bill III was graduating from high

school, we asked Bill II for help. He told Bill III, as

long as I'm his mother, he will not help him. SNAP!!

How do you turn down a son with a 4.5 GPA, when

all he wanted was to make him proud?

They made peace before he died in 2016,

and before he passed, he took Rachel to a Target

store and bought two baskets of merchandise for

her and his granddaughters. She said she felt like

Cinderella. Rachel said a beautiful speech at his

funeral. All his girlfriends were present and

accounted for. I gave my regards to his wife; I told

her I apologized for having children from her

husband. I apologized for not honoring their

marriage. I reminded the audience that, in this life, you reap what you sew; what goes around comes around, and it had come full circle for me. I wanted them to see this act of flesh on parade, and I was sorry. It was certainly a turning point in my life, in major proportions. The life lesson I learned is if at all possible, love myself and somehow redeem myself from Satan's grip.

***

My marriage to Bryce, Sr. was a mistake. My son is a blessing, and my granddaughter, Genesis is a double blessing. I can look back and see how different my life would have been if I had made different choices. My relationship with him was a nightmare in every sense of the journey. You can never recover twenty-one years of stolen time, but I don't regret the efforts of helping a human being obtain his freedom. There is a noble sentiment in that. Frankly, that's the only purpose I can summarize that was the original purpose. There are many brothers and sisters in prisons all over the world who are well-deserving of help and freedom.

We have to be careful when we put a decision on God that is not his direction or decision at all, but our own desires to be right, and we put Him as co-signer, when in reality, it's our own flesh, lust and the spirit of pride.

It's true when it is said 'pride goes before a fall' and 'a haughty spirit before destruction.' My fall took twenty-one years to manifest, and when it came, it came hard. The world as I knew it was over, and my peace and security as I knew it was nowhere to be found.

When I chose to inquire of the Lord about this, it was clear that I had created the hell I was in. It was my disobedience on that morning in North Hollywood, I TOLD YOU NO Although I felt, because I was a well-respected minister, I could manipulate this into what looked like a union that God had blessed, and I was so wrong.

When the lady from the Foursquare Church came to me and told me that the Lord didn't want me to get a divorce, I felt at that point we were in his will, but to my shame God was making me feel the full weight of my decision, He saw the future of GOAG, and in order to get the great harvest of souls this testimony will bring, my life had to be lived out in its entirety.

As for Bryce's Sr. girlfriend, two weeks after the fight, the Holy Spirit compelled me go back to the woman's house. When I drove up to the house, I spotted her son and asked him if he would get his mother. Before he could, she came out of the house and approached my car. I had gotten out by then, and the first thing I saw was fear in her eyes. I want to believe it was because I won the fight and she might fear she was in for another beating. It was none of that; it was because she had gotten the revelation that this was something more spiritual. The first thing I said was, "You hit *me*." She immediately apologized, and I accepted.

I told her that I didn't come to disturb her house, but she tore mine in two. I told her she had no clue of the pain he caused to hundreds of people who cared for me. I also told her if I offered her any advice, it would be that she should get to know a man before she moved him into her house, around her children, and married men are dangerous. I got a nerve, givin' her advice! I said I was a minister and I had no business out on Main Street, in a fight with my husband's girlfriend, and that I could have been arrested for domestic terrorism. For that, I was sorry. Then I told her I had a ministry called GIRLFRIEND OF A GANGBANGER, INC., and I hoped to see her in it someday. We embraced, and I left.

I got the news that she left him two weeks later, in an empty section 8 apartment, for another man. This, of course, was of no consequence to me. However, I always believed I could have given him the space he needed for a season. I wore big girl panties, and twenty eight years was a long time, but that's not where he was. He had intended what he manifested.

As far as my grandmother was concerned, when the divorce was final, I went to see her and she told me, "He never meant you well." Wow, this was my ninety-five year old Madear, and that was all she said on the subject, and it was enough.

I began to put the pieces back together. It was a process I didn't want to face, and if I didn't, it would cost me my life. The first thing I did was call a family friend named Ms. B, and she took me to The Dream Center in Los Angeles, California. I was willing to go into the recovery in the center, but God saw fit to give me a home. Von and Ms. B gave me an apartment that was very comfortable, I might add.

I knew I had unclean sprits and was flirting with mental illness at this point. I was willing to do whatever it took, to be whole. I had to let go of my pride, I had to humble myself, humble myself in the sense of asking for help. Life had humbled me, but in order to recover, my humility had to come from a place of knowing I needed help. No lifted up spirits could be in the way. I needed grace and mercy, more than anything else.

I was always saying he destroyed my name, my reputation that took me years to build, but in the big picture of things, I have no name. If I'm a representative of Christ, it's His name that was all I needed to call on. That's all I knew, church, and I wasn't ready to abandon what I believe is the truth. I didn't need programs at first. I needed healing in my soul, and in His name, I could find my way back again, the prodigal daughter home!

In my healing God opened up a mighty door, Ms. B's witchcraft was getting out of hand, I had to get away to keep from having a second stroke. I moved back to my son and daughters house, in San Jacinto California. It was as wild as before, but at least theses were familiar sprits? I was steadfast in seeking God for my escape this time I needed a permeate solution? Along with a Pastor friend of mine we went on a 50 day fast, something I never tackled before, on or around the 40th day I heard the Holy Ghost say IM GOING TO BLESS YOU, I had my idea of what I wanted, He also **said he would show me things I knew not of. Jeremiah 33:11.** However the blessing I received was far greater than I expected, In April 2020, I received a phone call from a gentleman, his conversation went something like this, I have an apartment for you, the application you filled out for senior housing seven years ago has come to my desk, I fell to the floor on my knees!!!, he told me that I would only pay what my income could afford...needless to say I only had an income of $200..00, This is the time corona virus was putting everyone on lock down, at that very moment I realize that the God I served is not quarantine or restricted by anything or anyone BUT ME. I didn't realize it was my submission to his will keeping me from seeing my true purpose,

Romans 12:1-1 I beseech you brethren by the mercies of God that you present your bodies a living sacrifice holy and acceptable unto God which is your reasonable service

My Life has changed 180 degrees' he has increased my station in life as well as enlarging my territory spiritually and financially. You have to take God at his word......

I have found that people who are in dire straits find themselves at risk for mental illness, homelessness, addicted to all kind of drugs, and slowly losing the ability to deal socially with people because the enemy always tells us it's somebody's else fault we are in the situation we find ourselves in. My last visit to The Dream Center, Pastor Matt. Opened the Bible to Isaiah 43, 18, (*the scripture that opened my life to Jesus Christ on January 18, 1984, when Rachel was in the hospital*) He began to say, "There is a lady here who believes she has lost her ministry, and God told me to tell you, you have not."

Oh my God, I knew he was talking to me. I had told God I didn't want the ministry, all I wanted was my relationship with Him. Nothing was more important to me. I was dirty, and I knew it, but he had revealed to me that it will be what he intended for me in the first place. Finally, I was living in my DIVINE purpose. I spent one year seeking my healing and deliverance, finally free from six Norcos and day drinking, to drown my enormous heartache, free from Somas and free from the disgrace and humiliation and what people thought of me, free from unhealthy soul ties. Now I can walk in my truth, face life as it comes, make mistakes, and they won't affect me in an abnormal way. And I am a pretty nice person and beautiful as well. If I were to sum it up, it would be in a poem.

Wise wretch!

With pleasure to refine, to please, with too much sprit to be e'er at ease...

You purchase pain with all that joy can give

And die of nothing but a rage to live!!

Author Unknown

My truth is simple. For all have sinned and come short of the glory of God. He has forgiven me for all that I have done, and that grace is sufficient. So I get up every day, thanking God for another day that I have breath in my body and that He has wonderfully and fearfully made me. Even when I had a stroke he Healed me beautifully ,he rejoices over me when I walk in his divine purpose my name GAIL- means THE FATHER REJOICES, I finally know who I am and what my purpose is on earth. And when my story is read the world over, in many languages, it will bless many people to see that the "KINGDOM OF GOD DWELLS IN YOU AND YOU

MUST TAKE IT BACK BY FORCE." A song by Aretha Franklyn simply says Ain't no way for me to love you if you won't let me, God can't show his Great Love he has for you if you won't let him." IT MUST BE DONE HIS WAY THRU HIS SON JESUS CHRIST"

Whether we know it or choose to ignore it, Los Angeles means lost angels. If you're, not careful you can lose your precious life. Your life is not a two-hour movie; it's a story to be lived one day a time, and you must choose how you're going to live it. While healing from my numerous breakdowns—nervous, emotional, mental, and full-blown menopause—I left Bryce Sr. with this message:

Now I lay me down to sleep, I pray my husband's soul you'll keep. If he dies before he wakes, I pray at peace my soul will stay... but if his sin is hidden within, let him rise to begin again. I FORGIVE YOU

GOAG INC.

When my life is over, all I want you to say about me is just call me FORGIVEN!!!

To my mother, my father and Hercy, this book was written as a testament of all of our lives and God's forgiveness. I love you all dearly and I will see you all in eternity.

Gail

About the Author

Gail Reed West is the director of the GIRLFRIEND OF A GANGBANGER INC. OUTREACH MINISTRY 501c3. She is single and the mother of four, grandmother of six, and great-grandmother of one. She was born and raised in South Central Los Angeles California and is a graduate of Phillips College of Northridge, California, where she received an Associate of Arts degree and a licensed cosmetologist. She is a retired social worker in the Black Infant Program of Riverside County. She has been honored as parent of the year in Fontana California. A published author, Gail is a profound orator and student of Biblical Studies; she received her license in Evangelism in 1992 from the PAW. She has several recognitions in Biblical courses. She is a Prophetic SEER' and Intercessor. She is a currently working on two new books, *90 Day Stroke-Out* and *Dirty Preachers*. Gail has traveled to many countries in Europe and plans to travel throughout the world, spreading the message of hope, healing and deliverance.

She has also served as president and minister of three women's ministries. Her journey will inspire you to challenge the Word of God, to find healing and peace, no matter the circumstances. She fought through molestation, drugs, promiscuity, dating a gang leader of the infamous *Crip Gang*, baby daddies, a sugar daddy, and she was a penitentiary wife for 21 years, only to emerge as a chosen vessel of light and truth, as an Ambassador of the Lord Jesus Christ, *'the baddest' gang leader she has ever met.'* Gail has committed her life to the Lordship of the Savior, her mission comes from *Matthew 11:12: The kingdom of God suffers violence, and the violent take it by force.*

Her manifesto comes from this mantra, KINGDOM MINDED for KINGDOM BUSINESS in KINGDOM AUTHORITY.

THE SEER

Places to find Gail:

Twitter: https://twitter.com/GailReedWest1

Email: GOAG91@yahoo.com

LinkedIn: https://www.linkedin.com/in/gail-reed-west-5ba79a46

Email: gailreed2005@gmail.com

Website: https://www.goaginc.org/about

E-mail gailreedwest@gmail.com

Pictorial Gallery

1974 mugshot of Raymond Washington

Born	Raymond Lee Washington August 14, 1953 Los Angeles, California, United States
Died	August 9, 1979 (aged 25) Los Angeles, California, United States
Known for	Criminal activity and founding the Crips

On August 9, 1979, Washington was murdered

My Ex-boyfriend.

Carolyn Gail Paula - @ Etta James After Party for Jenette 1976

"Billie" Billie Mattlock
(Mother of 7 - June 1940-February 1989)
(on the left)
Aunt Joyce (on the right) - Auntie Joyce- who gave
me my first personal book entitled "GOD I LISTEN"
By Eula H. MaClaney and introduced me to
beautiful clothes.

Montie
"Sam the Sham"

The Honorable Bishop R. W. McMurray and Evangelist Gail Reed West

My Children

Dream! #formyGenesis

My Daddy "Sam"

"If we confess our sins, he is faithful and just to forgive us our sins, and to cleanse us from all unrighteousness."
I John 1:9 (KJV)

#GOAGINC

"You cannot conquer what you can not confront."

Mr. Midget (1995-2007)

This is Billie, My Mom.

God answers prayers from a crying mother's heart.

First, Cynthia - Who listened when I was troubled, caught my tears when they were falling and friended me when I was lonely. My dearest cousin, sister and friend.

Thank you Princess for typing the original manuscript in 1996. That was a job.

Personal Contributing Editor,
Ms. Tamara King.

Made in the USA
Monee, IL
17 March 2021